The Interpretation of Financial Statements

THE CLASSIC 1937 EDITION

BY
BENJAMIN GRAHAM

AND
SPENCER B. MEREDITH

INTRODUCTION BY MICHAEL F. PRICE

HarperBusiness
A Division of HarperCollins*Publishers*

Library of Congress Cataloging-in-Publication Data

Graham, Benjamin. 1894–
    The interpretation of financial statements : the classic 1937 edition / Benjamin Graham and Spencer B. Meredith ; Introduction by Michael F. Price. — 1st HarperBusiness ed.
        p.   cm.
    0-88730-913-5
    1. Financial statements. I. Meredith, Spencer B. II. Title
HG4028.B2G72   1998
657'.3—DC21   98-12275

05 06 07 08   20 19 18 17 16

INTRODUCTION

In the spring of 1975, shortly after I began my career at Mutual Shares Fund, Max Heine asked me to look at a small brewery—the F&M Schaefer Brewing Company. I'll never forget looking at the balance sheet and seeing a +/- $40 million net worth and $40 million in "intangibles". I said to Max, "It looks cheap. It's trading for well below its net worth. . . . A classic value stock!" Max said, "Look closer."

I looked in the notes and at the financial statements, but they didn't reveal where the intangibles figure came from. I called Schaefer's treasurer and said, "I'm looking at your balance sheet. Tell me, what does the $40 million of intangibles relate to?" He replied, "Don't you know our jingle, 'Schaefer is the one beer to have when you're having more than one.'?"

That was my first analysis of an intangible asset which, of course, was way overstated, increased book value, and showed higher earnings than were warranted in 1975. All this to keep Schaefer's stock price higher than it otherwise should have been. We didn't buy it.

How many of today's jingles are carried on balance sheets? Billions? Or have things changed? Do companies like Coca-Cola, Philip Morris, and Gillette have huge "intangible" assets that they now leverage worldwide and don't even carry on their balance sheets?

This reissue of the classic 1937 edition of Ben Graham and Spencer Meredith's *The Interpretation of Financial*

Statements is right on time. Since our accounting conventions have been and continue to be both inadequate and constantly changing to keep up with the evolution of businesses, the basic study of financial statements by the average investor (businesspeople and school teachers, for example), is more important than ever.

In 1998, we are twenty years into a huge merger wave where most well-known large companies have acquired one or more other businesses. These companies' financial statements have become, as a result, harder and harder to true up. Currently the Financial Accounting Standards Board is studying whether to eliminate the pooling of interest method of accounting for acquisitions; this change would increase the amount of goodwill put on balance sheets. Pooling allows a company to combine its accounts with those of a merged or acquired company without listing goodwill. Pooling also restricts stock buybacks, while the purchase method of accounting (the other method of accounting in a merger or acquisition) allows stock buybacks and requires that any goodwill be amortized over a period not to exceed forty years. The request to record goodwill could result in lower acquisition premiums and corporate valuation levels.

Wells Fargo and First Interstate, two banks that merged in 1996, used purchase accounting while the recent Chase Manhattan Bank and Chemical Bank merger used the pooling method. In examining the results going forward from those mergers and others like them that the accounting methods need to be interpreted consistently. For example, Wells Fargo is using cash flow to buy back stock even after almost $300 million per year in goodwill amortization and now reports "cash earnings", as well as regular earnings, after amortization earnings per share. We at Mutual Shares look harder at "cash earnings" than earnings after amortization of goodwill in those industries where we see many deals and much goodwill created. The accurate interpretation on the part of investors of these accounting issues and corporate behavior changes is key in today's fast-paced market. Ben Graham's principle of always returning to the financial statements will keep an investor from making huge mistakes, and without huge mistakes the power of compounding can take over.

Whether you are a disciple of Ben Graham, a value investor, or a growth or momentum investor, you can agree that a stock's price must relate to its financials. From time to time investors ignore basic numbers like book value, cash flow, interest, and various ratios that fundamentally value common stock. It is especially common during periods of exuberance or fear that investors depart from the fundamental methods of successful investing. A sound understanding of how to read the basic financials should keep investors focused and thereby avoid costly mistakes, and also helps to uncover the hidden values of Wall Street.

Contemporary businesses are vastly more global than ever. Many of their globally distributed products are the result of decades of research and millions of dollars in promotions, yet they don't mention any intangibles on the balance sheet, because they're reflected in the market price. But how much will the market pay for a brand name, and why? Does the amount relate to the cash flows these well-known products produce? Global companies have gotten pretty good at leveraging their brands. Airlines are using computers for optimum load factors. Management information systems are helping to produce greater returns from assets than ever before. As companies globalize both directly, and through joint ventures, the true values of the name brands will take shape. Investors using financial statements can then determine how much the market is assigning to their "product" and "brand name" intangibles.

The Interpretation of Financial Statements was first published in 1937, shortly after the Ben Graham bible, *Security Analysis*, and during an era when investors left the stock market in droves. Today, when the contrary is the case, investors should confirm their understanding of the financial statements of the companies whose stock they own. This manual takes you through both the balance sheet (what a company owns and owes) and the income statement (what it earns). Helpful discussions of other statements, ratios, and a glossary of frequently used terms are also included.

Earnings reports, annual reports, and news releases concerning charges, reserves, and restatement of earnings, to name just a few subjects, will all become clearer with this book in hand. All investors, from beginners to old hands, should gain from the use of this guide, as I have. As Ben put it, in the end you should buy your stocks like you select your groceries, not your perfume. Focus on the fundamentals—how much you are paying for the steak and how much for the sizzle—and you shouldn't go wrong.

With *The Interpretation of Financial Statements* always at your side, I'm confident you will not get burned.

Good Luck Investing,
Michael F. Price

THE INTERPRETATION OF
FINANCIAL STATEMENTS

The Interpretation of Financial Statements

BENJAMIN GRAHAM

Head of Security Analysis Division,
New York Stock Exchange Institute
Lecturer in Finance, Columbia University

AND

SPENCER B. MEREDITH

Instructor in Security Analysis,
New York Stock Exchange Institute

WITH THE COLLABORATION OF

HAROLD T. JOHNSON
BIRL E. SHULTZ
ALBERT P. SQUIER
BELMONT TOWBIN
ERIC C. VANCE
of the New York Stock Exchange Institute

HARPER & BROTHERS PUBLISHERS
NEW YORK AND LONDON
1937

CONTENTS

PREFACE

This book is designed to enable you to read financial statements intelligently. Financial statements are intended to give an accurate picture of a company's condition and operating results, in a condensed form. Everyone who comes in contact with corporations and their securities has occasion to read balance sheets and income statements. Every business man and investor is expected to be able to understand these corporation statements. For security salesmen and for customers' men in particular, the ability to analyze statements is essential. When you know what the figures mean, you have a sound basis for good business judgment.

Our plan of procedure is to deal successively with the elements that enter into the typical balance sheet and income account. We intend first to make clear what is meant by the particular term or expression, and then to comment briefly upon its significance in the general picture. Wherever possible we shall suggest simple standards or tests which the investor may use to determine whether a company's showing in a given respect is favorable or the reverse. Much of this material may appear rather elementary, and indeed the analysis of financial statements is a comparatively simple matter. But even in the elementary aspects of the subject there are peculiarities and pitfalls which it is important to recognize and guard against.

Of course the success of an investment depends ultimately upon future developments, and the future may never be forecast with accuracy. But if you have precise information as to a company's present financial position and its past earnings record, you are better equipped to gauge its future possibilities. And this is the essential function and value of security analysis.

The following material is used in the courses in Security Analysis given by the New York Stock Exchange Institute. It is designed either for independent study as an elementary work, or as an introduction to a more detailed treatment of the subject. At the New York Stock Exchange Institute this material is employed in conjunction with the more advanced text, "Security Analysis," by Benjamin Graham and David L. Dodd.

New York City　　　　　　　　　　　　B. G.
May 2, 1937　　　　　　　　　　　　　S. B. M.

PART I

BALANCE SHEETS
AND INCOME ACCOUNTS

CHAPTER I

BALANCE SHEETS IN GENERAL

A balance sheet shows how a company stands at a given moment. There is no such thing as a balance sheet covering the year 1936; it can only be for a single date, for example, December 31, 1936. A single balance sheet may give some indications as to the company's past, but this may be studied intelligently only in the income accounts and by a comparison of successive balance sheets.

A balance sheet attempts to show how much a corporation has and how much it owes. What it has is shown on the asset side; what it owes is shown on the liability side. The assets consist of the physical properties of the company, money it holds or has invested, and money that is owed to the company. Sometimes there are also intangible assets, such as good-will, which are frequently given an arbitrary value. The sum of these items makes up the total assets of the company, shown at the bottom of the balance sheet.

On the liability side are shown not only the debts of the company, but also reserves of various kinds and the equity or ownership interest of the stockholders. Debts incurred in the ordinary course of business appear as accounts payable. More formal borrowings are listed as bonds or notes outstanding. Reserves, as will be shown later, may sometimes be equivalent to debt, but frequently they are of a different character.

3

The stockholders' interest is shown on the liability side as Capital and Surplus. It is often said that these items appear as liabilities because they stand for money owed by the corporation to its stockholders. It may be better to consider the stockholders' interest as representing merely the *difference* between assets and liabilities, and that it is placed on the liability side for convenience to make the two sides balance.

In other words, a balance sheet in the typical form:

Assets	$5,000,000	Liabilities	$4,000,000
		Capital & Surplus	1,000,000
	$5,000,000		$5,000,000

really means:

Assets	$5,000,000
Less Liabilities	4,000,000
Stockholders' Interest	$1,000,000

The total assets and the total liabilities are thus always equal on a balance sheet, because the capital and surplus items are worked out at whatever figure is needed to make the two sides balance.

CHAPTER II

DEBITS AND CREDITS

The understanding of financial statements will be aided by a brief outline of the bookkeeping methods upon which they are based. Bookkeeping, accounting, and financial statements, all are based on the two concepts of debit and credit.

An entry which increases an asset account is called a debit, or a charge. Conversely, an entry which decreases a liability account is also called a debit, or a charge.

An entry which increases a liability account is called a credit. Conversely, an entry which decreases an asset account is called a credit.

Since Capital and the various forms of Surplus are liability accounts, entries increasing these accounts are called credits and entries decreasing these accounts are called debits.

Business books are kept by what is called the "double-entry system," under which every debit entry is accompanied by a corresponding credit entry. Hence the books are always kept in balance, meaning that the total of asset accounts always equals the total of liability accounts.

The ordinary operations of a business involve various income and expense accounts such as Sales, Wages Paid, etc., which do not appear in the Balance Sheet. These operating or intermediate accounts are transferred (or "closed out") at the end of the period into Surplus or into Profit & Loss (which is the name given to the Surplus Account that reflects operating results, dividends, etc.). Since income entries are equivalent to additions to Surplus, they appear as credit or liability accounts. Expense entries, which are equivalent to deductions from Surplus, appear as debit or asset accounts.

A "trial balance" shows all the various accounts as they appear on the books before the intermediate or operating accounts are closed out into Profit & Loss. The total of all debit balances must be equal to the total of all credit balances.

The appended simplified "case history" may be found useful as indicating how the operations of a company are entered on the books, then reflect themselves in the trial balance, and finally are absorbed into the Balance Sheet. (It is not to be expected that corporate bookkeeping can be adequately treated within the confines of this presentation. Hence, the reader may wish to replace or supplement the following material by reference to some standard textbook on accounting.)

At the beginning of the period Company X showed the following Balance Sheet:

Cash	$3,000	Capital Stock	$5,000
Inventory	4,000	Profit & Loss Surplus	2,000
	$7,000		$7,000

The ledger (the book in which the accounts are kept), from which the above balance sheet was taken, would appear as follows:

Cash		*Inventory*		*Capital Stock*		*P & L Surplus*	
Dr.	Cr.	Dr.	Cr.	Dr.	Cr.	Dr.	Cr.
$3,000		$4,000			$5,000		$2,000

During the period it sells goods on credit for $3,000

which cost it \$1,800, and incurs various expenses, paid in cash, totalling \$500.

The original entries, which are made in the "Journal," are as follows:

Dr. Accounts Receivable...	\$3,000		Cr. Sales ...	\$3,000
[1]Dr. Cost of Sales	...	1,800	Cr. Inventory	1,800
Dr. Expense	...	500	Cr. Cash ...	500
(various items)				

At the end of the period the above entries are transferred to the ledger, which will appear as follows:

Cash		[2] Inventory		Accts. Rec.		Sales	
Dr.	Cr.	Dr.	Cr.	Dr.	Cr.	Dr.	Cr.
3,000	500	4,000	1,800	3,000			3,000
	2,500 (to bal- ance)		2,200 (to bal- ance)				
3,000	3,000	4,000	4,000				
2,500		2,200					

Cost of Sales	Expenses	Capital Stock	P. & L. Surplus
1,800	500	5,000	2,000

From the above the following trial balance would be "taken off":

Cash	2,500	Capital Stock	5,000
Inventory	2,200	P & L Surplus	2,000
Accts. Rec.	3,000	Sales	3,000
Cost of Sales	1,800		
Expenses	500		
	10,000		10,000

The operating accounts are then "closed out" into Profit & Loss by the following transfer entries:

Dr.	Sales	3,000	Cr.	Profit & Loss	3,000
Dr.	Profit & Loss	1,800	Cr.	Cost of Sales	1,800
Dr.	Profit & Loss	500	Cr.	Expenses	500

[1] Cost of Sales is actually calculated by deducting closing inventory from opening inventory plus purchases. We use the above entry for the sake of simplicity.

[2] See previous footnote.

It will be noted that these result in a net increase of $700 in Profit & Loss Surplus, representing the profit for the period. These entries eliminate the operating accounts. The ledger would now appear as follows:

```
     Cash                      Inventory                      Accts. Receivable
3,000    500              4,000    1,800                           3,000
         2,500 (to balance)        2,200 (to balance)
         ─────                     ─────
3,000    3,000           4,000    4,000
         ═════                     ═════
2,500                    2,200
            Sales        Cost of Sales                Expenses
to P & L 3,000   3,000   1,800   1,800 to P & L    500      500 to P & L
         ─────                   ─────
         3,000   3,000   1,800   1,800             500      500
                 ═════           ═════                      ═════
   Capital Stock      P & L Surplus
        5,000         (from cost of sales)  1,800   2,000
                      (   "   expenses)       500   3,000 (from sales)
                      To balance            2,700
                                            ─────
                                            5,000   5,000
                                            ═════
                                                    2,700
```

From the above ledger we would then have the following balance sheet, representing the condition of the company at the close of the period under consideration:

Assets		Liabilities	
Cash	2,500	Capital Stock	5,000
Inventory	2,200	P & L Surplus	2,700
Accts. Rec.	3,000		
	7,700		7,700

CHAPTER III

TOTAL ASSETS AND TOTAL LIABILITIES

The totals of assets and liabilities appearing on the balance sheet supply only a rough indication of the size of the company. Balance sheet totals may be readily inflated by excessive values set upon intangibles, and in many cases also the fixed assets are carried at a highly exaggerated figure. On the other hand, we find that in the majority of strong companies the good will which constitutes one of their most important assets either does not appear upon the balance sheet at all or is given but a nominal valuation (usually $1). There has recently developed a new practice of writing down the fixed assets, or plant account, to virtually nothing, in order to save depreciation charges. Hence it is a common occurrence to find that the true value of a company's assets is entirely different from the balance sheet total.

The size of a company may be measured in terms either of its assets or of its sales. In both cases the significance of the figure is entirely relative, and must be judged against the background of the industry. The assets of a small railroad will exceed those of a good-sized department store. From the investment standpoint—especially that of the buyer of high-grade bonds or preferred stocks—it may be well to attach considerable importance to large size. This would be true particularly in the case of industrial companies, for in this field the smaller enterprise is more subject to sudden adversity than is likely in a railroad or public utility. Where the purchase is made for speculative profit, or long-term capital gains, it is not so essential to insist upon dominant size, for there are countless examples of smaller companies prospering more than large ones. After all, the large companies themselves presented the best speculative opportunities while they were still comparatively small.

CHAPTER IV

CAPITAL AND SURPLUS

As stated before, the interest or equity of the stockholders in the business, as shown by the books, is represented by Capital and Surplus. In the simple case, formerly typical of every business, the money paid in by the stockholders is designated as Capital, and the profits not paid out as dividends make up the Surplus. The capital is represented by shares of stock, sometimes of only one kind or class, sometimes of various kinds which are usually called Preferred or Common. Other titles have also come into use—such as Class A or Class B, deferred shares, founders shares, etc. The rights and limitations of various kinds of stock cannot safely be inferred from their title, but the facts must be definitely ascertained from the charter provisions, which in turn are summarized in the investors' manuals or other statistical records and reference books.

The shares may be either of a certain par value or without par. In the simple case again, the par value shows how much capital was paid in for each share by the original subscribers to the stock. A company with one million shares, par $100, would presumably represent a far greater investment than another company with one million shares, par $5. However, in the modern corporate set-up neither the par value of each share nor the total dollar value of the capital stock may be in the slightest degree informing. The capital figure is frequently stated at much less than the actual amount paid in by the stockholders, the balance of their contribution being stated as some form of surplus. The shares themselves may be given no par value, which means that theoretically they represent no particular amount of money contribution, but rather a certain fractional interest in the total equity. In many cases nowadays a low par value is arbitrarily assigned to the shares, largely to reduce incorporation fees and transfer taxes.

These various practices may be illustrated by assuming that the stockholders of a company pay in $10,000,000 in exchange for 100,000 shares of capital stock. Under former procedure the shares would undoubtedly have been given a par value of $100, and the balance-sheet would have shown the following:

Capital—100,000 shares, par $100............... $10,000,000

More recently, the shares might have been given no par value, and the entry would have read:

Capital—100,000 shares, no par. Stated value...... $10,000,000

Or else the incorporators might have decided arbitrarily to state the capital at a smaller figure, say one-half of the amount paid in. In that case, the entries would read:

Capital—100,000 shares, no par. Stated value....... $5,000,000
Capital Surplus (or Paid-In Surplus).............. 5,000,000

The most "modern" arrangement would be to give the shares an arbitrarily low par, say $5. Hence we would see the following peculiar balance-sheet set-up:

Capital—100,000 shares, par $5.................. $ 500,000
Capital Surplus................................. 9,500,000

In present-day balance sheets, therefore, the division between Capital and Surplus may be quite meaningless. For most purposes of analysis it is best to take the capital and the various kinds of surplus items together, giving a single figure for the total equity of the stockholders.

CHAPTER V

PROPERTY ACCOUNT

The property account of a corporation includes land, buildings, equipment of all kinds, and office furnishings. These are often referred to as the "fixed assets" —although many are quite movable, such as locomotives, floating equipment, small tools, etc. Formerly it was customary to list the property account at the head of the asset side of the balance sheet, but it has now become frequent practice to list the cash and other current assets first and the fixed assets at the bottom. The proportion of the total assets taken up by the property account varies widely with different types of businesses. The property investment of a railroad is very large, while the property account of a patent drug company may be but a small part of the total assets. For example, the property account of Atchison, Topeka & Santa Fe Railway is over 88% of the total assets, while that of the Lambert Company is less than 15% of the total assets.

Established accounting practice requires that assets be shown at their actual cost, or at their fair value if this is definitely lower than cost. If an asset is definitely worth more than cost, it may be revalued at the higher figure. It is usually a difficult matter to determine the fair value of the fixed assets, as there is seldom a ready market for them. Hence most corporations regularly state their property account at cost, regardless of whether this represents its fair value at the time of the statement. In some cases, however, the property account is revalued as of a given date, and thus may appear on the balance sheet at a lower or higher figure than cost.

In some cases, also, arbitrary values have been placed on the fixed assets—values which bear little relation to the actual cost of their subsequent fair value. For example, the property account of the United States Steel Corporation was originally marked-up or inflated by an amount in excess of $600,000,000. This gave the common stock a fictitious book value, which of course far exceeded the initial market price of the shares. The epithet "watered stock" was commonly applied to inflated capitalizations of this kind. (Subsequently most of the "water" was written off the property account of United States Steel by various kinds of special charges against earnings and surplus.)

It is clear that the values at which the fixed assets are carried must not be taken too seriously. The unreliability of these entries has in fact impelled public opinion to the other extreme, and we find that buyers of securities in general now pay practically no attention to the property account, and relatively little attention to the balance sheet as a whole except as regards the working capital position. Preponderant emphasis is now laid upon the earnings record. We suggest that the property account be neither accepted at face value nor entirely ignored, but that reasonable consideration be given to it in appraising the company's securities.

CHAPTER VI

DEPRECIATION AND DEPLETION

All of the fixed assets, except land, are subject to a gradual loss of value through age and use. The allowance made for this loss of value is known variously as depreciation, obsolescence, depletion, and amortization. Depreciation applies to the ordinary wearing out of buildings and equipment. The amount of the depreciation to be charged each year is based on the value of the property (usually taken at cost), its expected life, and the salvage or scrap value when it is retired.

Example: If machinery is installed at a cost of $100,000, with an expected life of six years, and a probable final salvage value of $10,000, then the annual depreciation charge would be 1/6 of $90,000 ($100,000 less $10,000). This gives $15,000 as the annual depreciation charge.

Equipment for industries in which new inventions or improvements often appear soon becomes obsolete, even though it may still be serviceable. Thus in such industries as automobiles and chemicals, a charge for obsolescence may properly be added to the usual depreciation. In such cases a single figure is usually given for the two items.

Typical depreciation rates for important kinds of property include: Buildings 2 to 5%; Machinery 7 to

20%; Furniture and Fixtures 10 to 15%; Automobiles and Trucks 20 to 25%, etc.

The depreciation allowance for the year appears as a charge or deduction in the income account. It also appears in the balance sheet as an addition to the accumulated reserve for depreciation. The depreciation reserve may be stated either as a direct deduction from the fixed assets, on the left hand side, or as an offsetting account on the liability side.

The original or adjusted cost of the property, without allowance for depreciation, is called the gross value. This cost less accrued depreciation is called the net value. When property is retired its gross value is deducted from the property account, and the depreciation accrued against it to date is taken out of the depreciation reserve. This explains why the depreciation reserve on the balance sheet does not increase each year by the full amount charged for depreciation against earnings. If property is retired before it has been fully depreciated there is sustained a "loss on property retired" which is ordinarily charged to surplus (and not against the current year's earnings).

Depletion is an allowance similar to depreciation to cover the value of natural resources taken out of the ground. It is met with in mining, oil, and natural gas companies. Depletion charges are subject to a number of legal and accounting technicalities. Hence it is quite difficult to determine whether the depletion charge shown in a report is a fair one from the standpoint of the investor in the securities. A full discussion of the subject of depreciation and depletion charges should fall outside the scope of this book. Something will be said, however, regarding excessive and inadequate charges in the later sections devoted to the income account. (Chapter XXX.)

The amounts charged for depletion may be paid out to the stockholders each year as part of the dividend. Such payments are technically designated as "return of capital," and as such would ordinarily not be taxable to the stockholder as income.

CHAPTER VII

NON-CURRENT INVESTMENTS

Many companies have important investments in other enterprises, in the form of securities or advances. Some of these investments are of the same sort as are made by the ordinary buyer of securities, namely readily marketable bonds and stocks which are held for income or market profit and which may be sold at any time. Such investments are usually listed among the current assets, as "marketable securities."

Other investments, however, are made for purposes related to the company's business. They consist of stocks or bonds of affiliated or subsidiary companies, or loans or advances made to them. A consolidated balance sheet eliminates the securities held in *wholly owned* subsidiary companies, including instead the actual assets and liabilities of the subsidiaries as if they were part of the parent company. But *partly owned* subsidiary and affiliated enterprises may appear even in consolidated balance sheets under the heading of "non-current investments and advances."

These items are usually shown on the balance sheet at cost, though they frequently are reduced by reserves set up against them, and in fewer cases are increased to allow for accumulated profits. It is difficult to estimate the true value of these investments. Where it appears from the balance sheet that these items are likely to be of importance, a special effort should be made to obtain additional information regarding them.

Some investments stand midway between ordinary marketable securities and the typical non-marketable permanent commitment in a related company. This intermediate type is illustrated by du Pont's enormous holdings of General Motors, or the large investment of Union Pacific in the securities of various other railroads. Such holdings will appear among the miscellaneous assets rather than the current assets, since the companies regard them as permanent investments; but for some purposes (e.g.—calculating the quick assets per share of stock) it is permissible to regard them as the equivalent of readily marketable securities.

CHAPTER VIII

INTANGIBLE ASSETS

Intangible assets, as the name implies, are those which cannot be touched or weighed or measured. The most common intangibles are good-will, trademarks, patents and leaseholds. Somewhat distinct from the concept of good-will proper is the concept of going-concern value—the special profit-making character that attaches to a well established and successful business. Trademarks and brands constitute a rather definite type of good-will, and they are generally referred to as part of the good-will picture. An investor should recognize a very strong distinction between good-will as it appears—or, more generally, fails to appear—on the balance sheet, and good-will as it is measured and reflected by the market price of the company's securities.

The treatment of good-will on the balance sheet varies to an extraordinary extent among different companies. The most usual practice nowadays is either not to mention this asset at all, or to carry it at the nominal figure of $1. In some cases good-will has actually been acquired at a definite cost by purchase from former owners of the business, and it is then feasible to show the good-will at cost in the same manner as other assets. More often the good-will is entered originally on the books at some entirely arbitrary figure, which is more likely to exceed than to understate its fair value at the time.

The modern tendency is not to ascribe any value to good-will on the balance sheet. Many companies which started with a substantial good-will item have written this down to $1 by making corresponding reductions in their surplus or even their capital accounts.

This writing down of good-will does not mean that it is actually worth less than before, but only that the management has decided to be more conservative in its accounting policy. This point illustrates one of the many contradictions in corporate accounting. In most cases the writing off of good-will takes place after the company's position has improved. But this means that the good-will is in fact considerably more valuable than it was at the beginning.

An example of this is F. W. Woolworth Co.

When Woolworth common stock was first sold to the public, the company valued its good-will at $50,-000,000 on the balance sheet. However, the market price of the stock at that time indicated that the good-will was worth only $20,000,000. Many years later the company wrote down its good-will (in several installments) to $1, charging this $50,000,000 of write-offs against accumulated surplus. But when the last write-off was made in 1925, the market price of the shares indicated that the public valued the good-will at over $300,000,000.

Patents constitute a somewhat more definite form of asset than good-will. But it is extremely difficult to decide what is the true or fair value of a patent at any given time, especially since we rarely know just to what extent the company's earning power is dependent on any patent that it controls. The value at which the patents are carried on the balance sheet seldom offers any useful clue to their true worth.

The "leasehold" item is supposed to represent the money value of long-term leases held at advantageous rentals—i.e., rentals at lower rates than similar space could be leased. But, in a period of declining real estate values, long-term leaseholds are just as likely to prove to be liabilities as assets, and the investor should be very chary of accepting any valuation ascribed to them.

In general, it may be said that little if any weight should be given to the figures at which intangible assets appear on the balance sheet. Such intangibles may have a very large value indeed, but it is the income account and not the balance sheet that offers the clue to this value. In other words, it is the earning power of these intangibles, rather than their balance sheet valuation, that really counts.

CHAPTER IX

PREPAID EXPENSES

Often a company pays in advance for a service it is to receive over a specified length of time. For example, it might rent a building and pay $50,000 in advance for a year's rent. On the balance sheet at the beginning of the year, it would show this $50,000 as an asset—Prepaid Rent. Then each month it would deduct one-twelfth of this amount from the surplus earnings of that month and deduct a corresponding amount from the prepaid rent figure. Thus, at the end of the year, the $50,000 prepaid rent would have been written down to nothing, and a balance sheet at that time would not show this item. A balance sheet at the middle of the year might show—Prepaid Rent.... $25,000.

Similarly, the company might pay in advance the interest on money which it has borrowed for a certain length of time. The full amount of the prepaid interest would be shown on the balance sheet at the beginning of the period, and this would gradually be written down during the time the company had the use of the borrowed money. Occasionally, taxes and salaries are actually paid in advance, and these items are handled in this same way. A contract for $40,000 worth of advertising throughout the year 1937 might be made and paid in advance. The balance sheet as of December 31, 1936, would show this $40,000 as Prepaid Advertising Expenses. These expenses would be gradually written off during 1937. Most companies carry insurance of one kind or another, the premiums on which of course are payable in advance. This prepaid insurance is shown on the balance sheet at the full amount at the beginning of the period covered by the insurance, and it is written down to nothing during the period covered by the premium.

Usually, the balance sheet of a large company shows all of those various prepaid items grouped together under one figure, as Prepayments or Prepaid Expenses. From the nature of prepaid expenses, it may readily be seen that they would not be apt to amount to more than a small proportion of the company's total assets. The item Prepaid Expenses is of little importance in analysing the balance sheet, except that it gives some information as to how the company's business is conducted.

CHAPTER X

DEFERRED CHARGES

Frequently expenses are incurred which the company prefers to write off over a period of time rather than deduct at once from the surplus earnings. Such expenses are set up on the asset side of the balance sheet as Deferred Charges. It would appear that deferred charges and prepaid expenses are very much alike. As a matter of fact, prepayments are a special type of deferred charge, where (1) the company has a legal right to collect the service paid for in advance, and (2) the charge is written off during the specified time of the service. Ordinarily deferred charges do not represent any legal right to collect the service for which the expense was incurred, and they are written off at whatever rate the earnings of the company warrant.

For example, the company which paid the $50,000 rent in advance (Chapter IX), also incurred $15,000 expenses in moving into the new building. Rather than deduct these expenses of moving from the earnings of the month in which the company moved, they might set the expenses up as a deferred charge to be written off in the course of time. The company receives the benefit of these moving expenses as long as it stays in the new building and so the management may decide to write this deferred charge off gradually.

Expenses incurred in organizing a new company are usually set up as a deferred charge—Organization Expense. In the same way the expense of issuing bonds—particularly the difference (discount) between par and the amount received by the company—may be shown as a deferred charge, entitled Unamortized Bond Discount. The latter item would then be written off gradually over the life of the bond issue. (In many cases, however, all the bond discount is charged immediately against surplus, or else the discount remaining may be written off at some arbitrary time.) The practice in regard to writing off other deferred charges is extremely variable.

These deferred charges, although shown on the asset side of the balance sheet, are not tangible assets. Indeed, ordinary deferred charges are nearly as intangible as good-will.

CHAPTER XI

CURRENT ASSETS

Current assets are those which are immediately convertible into cash or which, in the due course of business, tend to be converted into cash within a reasonably short time. (The limit usually set is a year.) Sometimes they are called liquid or quick or floating assets. Current assets group themselves into three broad classes (1) Cash and its equivalents, (2) Receivables, that is, money which is due the company for goods or services sold, (3) Inventories held for sale or for the purpose of conversion into goods or service to be sold. In the operation of the business these assets change gradually into cash. For example, in a later balance sheet the present inventory would have become cash and receivables, while the present receivables would probably have become cash. Current assets are usually shown on the balance sheet in the relative order of their liquidity.

To give the picture in somewhat more detail, the following list of current asset items is shown, grouped for convenience into the three classes mentioned above.

(1) *Cash and Equivalents.*

Cash on hand or in bank (including certificates of deposit)

Call Loans ⎫
Time Loans ⎭ (Secured by marketable securities)

Government and Municipal Securities

      Other Marketable Securities
      Special Deposits
      Cash surrender value of insurance policies

(2) *Receivables.*
      Accounts Receivable
      Notes Receivable
      Interest Receivable
      Due from agents
      Unmeasured services (public utilities)

(3) *Inventories.*
      Finished Goods (Salable)
      Work in progress (Convertible)
      Materials and supplies (Consumable)

Certain kinds of receivables may be relatively non-current—e.g., amounts due from officers and employees, including stock subscriptions. If such accounts are not due to be received by the company within a year, they are usually shown separately from the current assets.

On the other hand, it is customary to include the full amount of installment accounts receivable in the current assets, even though a good part may be due later than one year from the date of the balance sheet. Similarly, the entire merchandise inventory is included in the current assets, although some of the items may be slow-moving.

CHAPTER XII

CURRENT LIABILITIES

Corresponding to current assets, but on the other side of the balance sheet, are current liabilities. For the most part these are the debts contracted by the company in the ordinary course of operating the business, and presumably are payable within a year, at most. In addition, all other kinds of debts maturing within a year's time are included among the current liabilities. The more important kinds of current liabilities may be enumerated as follows:

Notes, bills, or loans payable (these include bank loans, commercial paper outstanding, etc.)
Acceptances payable
Accounts payable
Dividends and interest payable
Bonds, mortgages, or serial obligations due within a year, including those called for redemption
Advances (from customers, affiliates, stockholders, etc.)
Consumers deposits
Unclaimed checks and refunds
Accrued interest, wages, and taxes
Reserve for Federal taxes

CHAPTER XIII

WORKING CAPITAL

In studying what is called the "current position" of an enterprise, we never consider the current assets by themselves, but only in relation to the current liabilities. The current position involves two important factors: (a) the excess of current assets over current liabilities—known as the Net Current Assets or the Working Capital, and (b) the *ratio* of current assets to current liabilities—known as the Current Ratio.

The Working Capital is found by subtracting the current liabilities from the current assets. Working Capital is a consideration of major importance in determining the financial strength of an industrial enterprise, and it deserves attention also in the analysis of public utility and railroad securities.

In the working capital is found the measure of the company's ability to carry on its normal business comfortably and without financial stringency, to expand its operations without the need of new financing, and to meet emergencies and losses without disaster. The investment in plant account (or fixed assets) is of little aid in meeting these demands. Shortage of working capital, at its very least, results in slow payment of bills with attendant poor credit rating, in curtailment of operations and rejection of desirable business, and in a general inability to "turn around" and make progress. Its more serious consequence is insolvency and the bankruptcy court.

The proper amount of working capital required by a particular enterprise will depend upon both the amount and the character of its business. The chief point of comparison is the amount of working capital per dollar of sales. A company doing business for cash and enjoying a rapid turnover of inventory—for example, a chain grocery enterprise—needs a much lower working capital compared with sales than does the manufacturer of heavy machinery sold on long-term payments.

The working capital is also studied in relation to fixed assets and to capitalization, especially the funded debt and preferred stock. A good industrial bond or preferred stock is expected, in most cases, to be entirely covered in amount by the net current assets. The working capital available for each share of common stock is an interesting figure in common stock analysis. The growth or decline of the working capital position over a period of years is also worthy of the investor's attention.[1]

In the field of railroads and public utilities, the working capital item is not scrutinized as carefully as in the case of industrials. The nature of these service enterprises is such as to require relatively little investment in receivables or inventory (supplies). It has been customary to provide for expansion by means of new financing rather than out of surplus cash. A prosperous utility may at times permit its current

[1] A severe test of a company's financial position is applied by using the current assets exclusive of inventory. These may be called the Quick Assets, and their amount, less current liabilities, would be known as the Net Quick Assets. Normally there should be a comfortable excess of "Quick Assets" over all current liabilities.

liabilities to exceed its current assets, replenishing the working capital position a little later as part of its financing program.

The careful investor, however, will prefer utility and railroad companies that consistently show a comfortable working capital situation.

CHAPTER XIV

CURRENT RATIO

One of the most frequently used figures in analyzing balance sheets is the ratio between current assets and current liabilities. This is usually called the current ratio, and it is obtained by dividing the total current assets by the total current liabilities. For example, if the current assets are $500,000 and the current liabilities $100,000, the current ratio is 5 to 1, or simply 5. When a company is in a sound position, the current assets well exceed the current liabilities, indicating that the company will have no difficulty in taking care of its current debts as they mature.

What constitutes a satisfactory current ratio varies to some extent with the line of business. In general the more liquid the current assets, the less the margin needed above current liabilities. Railroads and public utilities have not generally been required to show a large current ratio—chiefly because they have small inventories and their receivables are promptly collectible. In industrial companies a current ratio of 2 to 1 has been considered a sort of standard minimum. It will be found, however, that nearly all the companies with listed securities far exceed this figure. The appended table gives recent aggregate current ratios for various industries.

The current ratio should be generally analyzed further by separating out the inventory. It is customary

CURRENT RATIO

End of 1935 Fiscal Year

Number of Companies	Industry	Ratio to 1	Number of Companies	Industry	Ratio to 1
18	Tobacco...............	14.4	14	Railroad Equipment....	5.2
7	Knit Goods...........	7.9	8	Containers............	5.1
5	Farm Equipment.......	7.7	15	Department Stores.....	5.0
8	Shoes and Leather.....	7.7	22	Iron and Steel........	4.9
8	Electrical Equip.......	7.4	7	Radio.................	4.6
20	Chemicals............	6.9	34	Automobile Parts.......	4.4
20	Household Products....	6.9	26	Mining (Misc.).........	4.3
12	Publishing............	6.9	7	Baking................	4.2
11	Office Equipment.......	6.6	4	Mail Order............	4.2
20	Building Equipment....	6.4	6	Paper.................	3.9
23	Manufacturing (Misc.)..	6.3	7	Grocery Chains........	3.8
8	Apparel...............	6.0	27	Petroleum.............	3.8
21	Industrial Mach........	6.0	8	Shipping..............	3.7
8	Variety Chains........	6.0	4	Silk Goods............	3.6
7	Meat Packing..........	5.9	7	Cotton Goods..........	3.5
5	Woolen Goods.........	5.9	4	Dairy Products........	3.5
13	Food Products........	5.7	13	Automobiles...........	3.0
9	Sugar.................	5.7	10	Coal..................	3.0
7	Aircraft...............	5.6	8	Motion Pictures........	2.8
13	Drugs & Cosmetics.....	5.5	22	Public Utilities........	1.9
9	Rubber & Tires........	5.3	25	Railroads.............	0.7

to require that the cash items and the receivables together exceed all the current liabilities. (There is a tendency now to apply the term "quick assets" to these current assets, exclusive of inventory.) If the inventory is of a readily salable kind, and particularly if the nature of the business makes it very large at one season and quite small at another, the failure of a company to meet this latter "quick asset test" may not be of great importance. In every such case, however, the situation must be looked into with some care to make sure that the company is really in a comfortable current position.

CHAPTER XV

INVENTORIES

There is a tendency to consider a large inventory as a bad thing for any business. This is not strictly true, since inventories are assets, and in general the more assets a company has the better off it is. Large inventories, however, often do create trouble of various kinds. They may require substantial bank borrowings to finance them, or else absorb an undue amount of the company's cash. They may lead to heavy losses in case of a decline in commodity prices. Theoretically, they could produce similar profits, but experience shows that such profits are not nearly as large or as frequent as the inventory losses. Finally an abnormally large inventory suggests that a good part of the merchandise may be unsalable and that its price may have to be drastically reduced in order to move it.

The inventory figure should be studied in relation to various factors. The chief criterion is the "turnover"—defined as the annual sales divided by the inventory.[1] The standards on this point vary widely for different industries. Some idea of the range of variation, and an indication also of what figure to require in individual cases, will be supplied by the following

---

[1] The true turnover is found by dividing the inventory into the cost of sales, but it is customary to use the total sales instead of the cost of sales. This accepted "turnover" is thus always larger than the true figure.

list of average ratios of sales to inventories for different lines:

INVENTORY TURNOVER—1934

(Annual Sales Divided by Year-End Inventory)

Number of Companies	Product	Rate	Number of Companies	Product	Rate
58	Silk goods.............	10.1	193	Department Stores.....	5.9
82	Shoe Mfg..............	9.4	39	Chemicals.............	5.6
39	Electrical Equipment...	8.7	34	Paper.................	5.5
54	Automobile Parts......	8.1	40	Leather Tanners.......	4.9
51	Cotton Goods.........	8.1	23	Shoes (Retail)	4.9
94	Paints and Varnishes...	7.6	33	Publishers.............	4.8
34	Hosiery...............	7.2	42	Hardware and Tools....	3.7
64	Furniture..............	6.0			

Where the sales are not available, it is more difficult to form a worthwhile opinion on the inventory factor. However, the figures may usefully be studied year by year and compared with each other, with the net profits, with the other current assets and with the working capital. The appended table shows the percentage of total current assets represented by inventory in various lines, as at the end of 1935.

INVENTORY TO TOTAL CURRENT ASSETS

Industry	Per-cent	Industry	Per-cent
Motion Picture	68.9	Industrial Machinery	42.0
Tobacco	68.2	Apparel	41.6
Woolen Goods	65.8	Building Equipment	41.0
Variety Chains	65.4	Automobiles	40.7
Grocery Chains	64.2	Food Products	39.5
Cotton Goods	59.0	Drugs and Cosmetics	38.7
Meat Packing	57.7	Farm Equipment	38.6
Iron and Steel	57.4	Office Equipment	37.1
Mail Order	56.1	Electrical Equipment	37.0
Rubber and Tires	53.3	Automobile Parts	35.6
Mining (Miscellaneous)	51.6	Chemicals	34.4
Paper	51.3	Aircraft	32.6
Shoes and Leather	49.8	Baking	31.8
Sugar	49.8	Dairy Products	29.2
Household Products	49.2	Coal	28.1
Petroleum	48.7	Publishing	27.8
Containers	46.5	Railroads	26.5
Knit Goods	46.4	Radio	25.6
Silk Goods	46.2	Radio Equipment	25.5
Manufacturing (Misc.)	44.8	Shipping	18.2
Department Stores	42.7	Public Utilities	17.6

CHAPTER XVI

RECEIVABLES

The relative amount of receivables varies widely with the type of industry and the trade practices in paying up accounts. Also in a given line of business receivables are apt to vary with the condition of bank credit, that is, when bank credit is strained the amount of receivables increases as the company extends more than the usual amount of credit to its customers.

As in the case of inventories, receivables should be studied in relation to the annual sales, where available, and in relation to changes shown over a period of years. If the receivables seem unusually large in proportion to sales, or to other items, there is some indication that an unduly liberal credit policy has been pursued, and that more or less serious losses are likely to be sustained from bad accounts.

Receivables require most careful scrutiny in the case of companies selling goods on a long term payment basis. Such concerns include department stores, credit chains, some mail order houses and makers of machinery and equipment of many kinds (e.g.—farm implements, trucks and office equipment). Much of this installment payment business is carried on through finance companies which advance funds against the notes or guarantee of the seller. Frequently the receivables of a manufacturing company are sold to the finance company with a "re-purchase agreement," in which case neither the receviables nor the debt to the finance company appear directly on the balance sheet of the manufacturing company, but are referred to in a footnote. In analyzing a balance sheet, such discounted receivables must be given full consideration, as the equivalent both of assets and liabilities.

CHAPTER XVII

CASH

No useful separation can be made between cash proper and the other "cash assets" or "cash equivalents," consisting of certificates of deposit, call loans, marketable securities, etc. For practical purposes the various kinds of cash assets may be considered as interchangeable. In theory a company should not keep any more cash on hand than is required for the transaction of its usual business and the possible needs that may suddenly arise. But for some years past there has been a widespread tendency towards holding more cash than the business seems to need. Much of this surplus cash is held in the form of marketable securities. The current return on these investments is usually small. They may yield substantial profits (or losses) due to market changes, but such operations are not properly part of the ordinary commercial or manufacturing business.

A shortage of cash is ordinarily taken care of by bank borrowings. In the usual case, therefore, a weak financial position is likely to be shown more through large bank loans than through insufficient cash on hand. During a period of depression it is particularly important to watch the cash account from year to year. Some companies build up their cash account even during a period of losses, by liquidating a large part of their other assets, especially inventories and receivables. Other concerns show a serious loss of cash, or—what amounts to the same thing—a substantial increase in bank loans. In such periods the way in which the losses reflect themselves in the balance sheet may be more important than the amount of the losses themselves.

Where the cash holdings are exceptionally large in relation to the market price of the securities, this factor usually deserves favorable attention. In such a case the common stock may be worth more than the earnings record indicates, because a good part of its value is represented by cash holdings which contribute little to the income account. Eventually, the stockholders are likely to get the benefit of these cash assets, either through their distribution or their productive use in the business.

CHAPTER XVIII

NOTES PAYABLE

The total amount of current liabilities is of interest only in relation to the current assets. You have already seen the importance of the current ratio (total current assets to total current liabilities) and the desirability of having the quick assets, exclusive of inventory, exceed the current liabilities.

The most important individual item among the current liabilities is that of Notes Payable. This generally represents bank loans, but it may also apply to trade accounts or borrowings from affiliated companies or from individuals. The fact that a company has borrowed from the banks is not in itself a sign of weakness. Seasonal borrowings, which are entirely paid off after the close of the active sales period, are considered desirable from the viewpoint both of the company and the banks. But more or less permanent bank loans, even though they may be well covered by current assets, are apt to be an indication that the company is in need of long-term capital in the form of bonds or stock.

Where the balance sheet shows notes payable the situation must always be studied with greater care than is otherwise called for. If the notes payable are substantially exceeded by the cash holdings they can ordinarily be dismissed as relatively unimportant. But if the borrowings are larger than the cash and receivables combined, it is clear that the company is relying heavily on the banks. Unless the inventory is of unusually liquid character, such a situation may justify misgivings. In such a case the bank loans should be studied over a period of years to see whether they have been growing faster than sales and profits. If they have, it is a definite sign of weakness.

CHAPTER XIX

RESERVES

It is useful to divide Reserves into three classes: (a) those representing a more or less definite liability, (b) those representing an offset against some asset, and (c) those which are really part of the surplus.

Reserves of the first class are set up for taxes, for accident claims and for other pending litigation, for refunds to customers, etc. These are for the most part true current liabilities, even though in some cases they are separated from the current liabilities in the balance sheet.

The most important *offsetting reserves* are those for depreciation and depletion, which we have already discussed. It will be remembered that these may be found either on the asset side, as a deduction from the property account, or on the liability side of the balance sheet. Another standard offsetting reserve is that for losses on receivables—or "reserve for bad accounts." This is usually deducted directly from the accounts and notes receivable, and frequently the amount so deducted is not stated.

A third important offset-reserve is that for decline in inventories. In dealing with such a reserve it is essential to know whether it reflects a decline that has already taken place or merely one that may be in the offing. If the former is true, the inventory must be considered as definitely reduced by the amount of the reserve. But if the reserve is set up to take care of a possible future decline in value, it must be viewed rather as a Reserve for Contingencies, which is in reality part of the Surplus. The same point may be made with respect to reserves against marketable securities and other investments. Here too it is important to know if they reflect a past and actual, or merely a possible, decline in value.

Contingency Reserves, and other similar reserves, tend to make corporate statements quite confusing, because they obscure the time and effect of various kinds of losses. If in one year a company sets up a reserve for future decline in inventory value, it seems proper to take this reserve out of surplus, rather than charge it to earnings, since the loss has not actually been realized. But if in the next year a decline in inventory takes place, it seems proper again to charge this loss against the reserve set up for that contingency. It follows that the loss, although actually incurred, is not charged against income in any year, and to that extent the earnings have been over-stated.

For example, if a company showed a $2,000,000 net income in its income account, but the balance sheet at the end of the year did not show a $6,000,000 reserve which had existed a year previous, it might be reasonable to conclude that the company in that year had really lost $4,000,000. Occasionally a reserve is transferred back to surplus. Of course if the $6,000,000 reserve had been transferred back to surplus, the surplus would show this increase and the company's net income or profit of $2,000,000 could be regarded as correct.

To avoid being deceived by these devices, the investor must examine both the income and the surplus account over several years, and make due allowance for any amounts charged to surplus or reserves which really represent business losses during the period. Also in industries where inventory reserves are frequently set-up (e.g., the rubber industry) the investor should be particularly careful not to exaggerate the significance of a single year's earnings.

Now and then the balance sheet contains items such as "Reserve for Plant Improvement," "Reserve for Working Capital," "Reserve for Preferred Stock Retirement," etc. Reserves of this sort represent neither a debt nor a definite deduction from any asset. They are clearly part of the surplus account. The purpose in setting them up is usually to indicate that these funds are not available for distribution to the stockholders. If this is so, such reserves may be considered as "Appropriated Surplus."

CHAPTER XX

BOOK VALUE OR EQUITY

The book value of a security is in most cases a rather artificial value. It is assumed that if the company were to liquidate, it would receive in cash the value at which its various tangible assets are carried on the books. Then the amounts applicable to the various securities in their due order would be their book value. (The word "equity" is frequently used instead of book value in this sense, but it is generally applied only to common stocks and to speculative senior securities.)

As a matter of fact, if the company were actually liquidated the value of the assets would most probably be much less than their book value as shown on the balance sheet. An appreciable loss is likely to be realized on the sale of the inventory, and a very substantial shrinkage is almost certain to be suffered in the value of the fixed assets. In practically every case the adverse conditions which would lead to a decision to liquidate the business would also make it impossible to obtain anywhere near cost or reproduction price for the plant and machinery.

The book value really measures, therefore, not what the stockholders could get out of their business (its liquidating value), but rather what they have put into the business, including undistributed earnings. The book value is of some importance in analysis because a very rough relationship tends to exist between the amount invested in a business and its average earnings. It is true that in many individual cases we find companies with small asset values earning large profits, while others with large asset values earn little or nothing. Yet in these cases some attention must be given to the book value situation, for there is always a possibility that large earnings on the invested capital may attract competition and thus prove temporary; also that large assets, not now earning profits, may later be made more productive.

CHAPTER XXI

CALCULATING BOOK VALUE

As has already been said, in calculating book value it is assumed that the company's assets are worth the figure shown on the balance sheet. Indeed, book value simply means the value as shown by the books or balance sheet.

To take a simple example, a company's balance sheet is as follows:

Fixed Property......	$1,000,000	Capital Stock.......	$1,700,000
Good-will..........	500,000	Surplus............	100,000
Current Assets......	500,000	Cur. Liabilities......	200,000
	$2,000,000		$2,000,000

In this case the capital stock is represented by 17,000 shares of $100 par value common stock. To find the book value of the common stock, add the $100,000 surplus to the $1,700,000 value shown for the stock, making a total of $1,800,000. Then look on the asset side of the balance sheet for intangibles. You will find $500,000 good-will. This is then deducted from the $1,800,000, leaving $1,300,000 equity available for the 17,000 common shares. Incidentally, the figure $1,300,000 is often referred to as the "net tangible assets" of the company. Dividing this out, the *net* book value per share would be $76.47.

If you had not deducted the intangibles and had simply divided the $1,800,000 by the 17,000 shares you would have found the book value per share to be $105.88. You will note that there is quite a difference between this book value and the *net* book value of $76.47 a share. If only "book value" of the stock is mentioned, *tangible* or *net* book value is usually meant. The larger figure may be termed: "Book value, including intangibles."

CHAPTER XXII

BOOK VALUE OF BONDS AND STOCKS

The balance sheet of a company having bonds, preferred and common stocks, might be as follows:

Fixed Property......	$1,000,000	7% Pfd. Stock	
Good-Will..........	500,000	($100 par)........ $	600,000
Current Assets......	500,000	*Common Stock	
		(No par).........	600,000
		1st Mortgage 6%	
		Bonds...........	500,000
		Cur. Liabilities......	200,000
		Surplus...........	100,000
	$2,000,000		$2,000,000

* 17,000 shares

To find the net book value (net tangible asset value) of the bonds you would add the figure for the bonds, plus the figures for the preferred stock, common stock and surplus, and from this total of $1,800,000, deduct the $500,000 good-will, leaving $1,300,000 of net tangible assets applicable to the $500,000 of bonds. Thus each $1,000 bond would have a net book value of $2,600.

To find the net book value of the preferred stock, the bonds are excluded and only the figures for the preferred, common and surplus are added and the good-will deducted as before, leaving $800,000 of net tangible assets applicable to the 6,000 shares of preferred stock, or $133.33 a share net book value.

The first step in finding the net book value of the

common stock in a case where there is a preferred stock, is to look up the liquidating value of the preferred stock. Frequently preferred stock is entitled to more than par in liquidation (or dissolution) and, of course, in the case of no par stock it is necessary to look up the liquidating value anyway. In this particular case the preferred stock has a liquidating value of $105, or a total $630,000. Next find the net tangible assets applicable to the preferred stock, $800,000 as above, and from this deduct the total liquidating value of the preferred stock, $630,000. The remaining amount, $170,000, is the net tangible assets applicable to the 17,000 shares of no par common stock, or $10 a share net book value.

If there are accumulated dividends on the preferred stock, these must also be deducted in calculating the book value of the common (or of a junior preferred issue). Sometimes allowance must be made for participating features of a preferred or Class A stock.

Sometimes, also, the value in case of dissolution is not representative of the claim on earnings, and it is better to value the preferred stock at some figure which fairly reflects its dividend rate. (This may be called its "effective par value.") For example, under present conditions, an $8 non-callable preferred stock, even though entitled to only $100 a share in case of dissolution, might properly be deducted at a 5% basis, or $160 a share, in order to determine the balance of assets available for the common stock.

CHAPTER XXIII

OTHER ITEMS IN BOOK VALUE

In calculating the book value of a security, the various forms of surplus are all treated simply as surplus. For example, a company might show Capital Surplus, Appropriated Surplus, Premium on Stock Sold, and Profit and Loss or Earned Surplus. These would all be added together and regarded as surplus.

In the chapter on Reserves, it was mentioned that certain kinds of reserves are really a part of the surplus. These include Reserves for Contingencies (unless they relate to a definite and reasonably probable payment or loss of value); General Reserve, Reserves for Dividends, Reserves for Preferred Stock Retirement, Reserves for Improvements, Reserves for Working Capital, etc. Reserves for Insurance may also properly be considered in the same class, but Reserves for Pensions are usually a true liability and should not be included as part of the surplus.

These reserves equivalent to surplus (sometimes called "Voluntary Reserves") which are really part of the surplus, should be added in with the surplus in figuring the book value. In finding the net book value all the intangibles should be deducted. Such deferred charges as organization expense and unamortized bond discount, should also be excluded.

CHAPTER XXIV

LIQUIDATING VALUE AND NET CURRENT
ASSET VALUE

Liquidating Value differs from Book Value in that it is supposed to make allowance for loss of value in liquidation. It is obviously impractical to talk of the liquidating value of a railroad or the ordinary public utility. On the other hand, the liquidating value of a bank, insurance company, or typical investment trust (or investment holding company) may be calculated with a fair to high degree of accuracy; and if the figure is well above the market price this fact may be of real importance.

In the case of industrial enterprises, the liquidating value may or may not be a useful concept, depending on the nature of the assets and the capitalization set-up. It is particularly interesting when the current assets make up a relatively large part of the total assets, and the liabilities ahead of the common are relatively small. This is true because the current assets usually suffer a much smaller loss in liquidation than do the fixed assets. In some cases of liquidation it happens that the fixed assets realize only about enough to make up the shrinkage in the current assets.

Hence the "net current asset value" of an industrial security is likely to constitute a rough measure of its liquidating value. It is found by taking the net current assets (or "working capital") alone and deducting

55

therefrom the full claims of all senior securities. When a stock is selling at much less than its net current asset value, this fact is always of interest, although it is by no means conclusive proof that the issue is under-valued.

CHAPTER XXV

EARNING POWER

Outside of the field of banks, insurance companies and, particularly, investment trusts, it is only in the exceptional case that book value or liquidating value plays an important role in security analysis. In the great majority of instances the attractiveness or the success of an investment will be found to depend on the earning power behind it. The term "Earning Power" should be used to mean the earnings that may reasonably be expected over a period of time in the future. Since the future is largely unpredictable, we are usually compelled to take either the current and past earnings as a guide, and to use these figures as a base in making a reasonable estimate of future earnings.

If there have been reasonably normal business conditions for a period of years, the average of the earnings over the period may afford a better index of earning power than the current figure alone. This is particularly true if the purpose is to determine whether a bond or a preferred stock constitutes a safe investment.

In the next few chapters the elements of an earnings statement will be discussed.

CHAPTER XXVI

TYPICAL PUBLIC UTILITY INCOME ACCOUNT

The following consolidated income account of a public utility holding company and its subsidiaries may be regarded as representative:

AMERICAN GAS AND ELECTRIC COMPANY

(YEAR ENDED DECEMBER 31, 1935)

Total Operating Revenue		$64,936,196
Operating Expenses	$20,379,243	
Maintenance	3,542,460	
Depreciation	8,730,973	
Taxes	8,664,795	
Operating Income		23,618,725
Other Income		728,672
Other Income (Parent Company)		279,629
Total Income		24,627,026
Expenses of Parent Company (Including Taxes)	467,265	
Balance Available for Fixed Charges		24,159,761
Subsidiary Preferred Dividends	3,104,342	
Interest and Other Deductions (Subsidiary)	7,936,175	
Interest and Other Deductions (Parent Company)	2,562,802	
Net Income		10,556,442
Preferred Dividends	2,133,738	
Common Dividends	6,267,073	
Surplus Additions:		
Sundry Credits		40,862
Surplus Deductions:		
Premium and Unamortized Discount and Expenses on Bonds Redeemed	306,441	
Elimination of Credit Balances in Surplus Accts. of Subsidiaries Liquidated	47,612	
Sundry Credits:		
Adjustment of Book Value of Stocks and Bonds of Other Companies	87,397	

Tax Payments for Prior Years.   33,496
Sundry Debits.   1,417
Increase in Surplus for Year.   1,720,509
Surplus for Previous Year.   66,609,188
Profit and Loss Surplus (Per Balance Sheet).   68,329,732

Some explanation of various items in this income account may be found helpful.

The Total Operating Revenue or Gross Revenue is frequently divided as to source—e.g., electric, gas, water, transportation, etc. The Operating Expenses include cost of materials, labor, administration (overhead), etc. Maintenance and Depreciation are discussed a little later. Taxes are frequently divided between local, state, and miscellaneous federal on the one hand, and federal income taxes on the other.

Other Income comes from sources other than regular sales to customers and usually refers to income from investments and—in the case of a holding company—charges for services of various kinds to the subsidiaries.

The other deductions included in the fixed charges comprise amortization of bonds and (sometimes) rentals for leased property.

Subsidiary preferred dividends are the dividends paid on preferred stock outstanding in the hands of the public—i.e., not held by the parent company. Similarly "minority interest" means the proportion of the earnings of subsidiaries applicable to the common stock owned by the public. (The majority of the common stock is of course owned by the holding company.)

The additions to surplus, not included in the income account proper, relate to income not strictly part of the year's operations, such as adjustments of past years' taxes and of reserves previously set up, refunds, etc.

Similarly, the deductions from surplus comprise such items as loss on sales of securities and on property retired, expense of issuing securities, bond discount written off in a lump sum, etc. Charges to surplus must always be scrutinized to see if they have a bearing on the actual earnings over a period of years.

CHAPTER XXVII

A TYPICAL INDUSTRIAL INCOME ACCOUNT

AMERICAN ROLLING MILL COMPANY
(YEAR ENDED DECEMBER 31, 1935)

Net Sales...		$76,799,000
Cost of Sales............................	$56,251,000	
Selling, General and Administrative Expense.	5,631,000	
Maintenance and Repairs...................	5,858,000	
Provision for Doubtful Accounts...........	174,000	
Rents and Royalties.......................	128,000	
Taxes (other than income).................	660,000	
Operating Income..........................		8,097,000
Other Income (Net)........................		1,391,000
Total Income..............................		9,488,000
Depreciation and Depletion................	2,076,000	
Income Taxes..............................	615,000	
Interest and Debt Discount................	2,483,000	
Minority Interest.........................	4,000	
Net Income................................		4,310,000
Preferred Dividends.......................	348,000	
Common Dividends..........................	1,068,000	
Miscellaneous Additions to Surplus........		130,000
Miscellaneous Deductions from Surplus.....	1,830,000	
Increase in Surplus for Year..............		1,194,000
Surplus from Previous Year................		14,634,000
Profit and Loss Surplus (12/31/35)........		15,828,000

Net Sales means sales less returns and allowances. Cost of Sales in this case means Factory Cost, including labor, materials, and factory overhead, except maintenance which is here stated separately. The other items in the income account are self-explanatory. In this case the preferred dividends include $12 per share, or $232,000, on account of accumulations. The regular annual preferred dividend requirements were only $116,000.

CHAPTER XXVIII

A TYPICAL RAILROAD INCOME ACCOUNT

All railroad reports are rendered on a uniform basis in accordance with the rules of the Interstate Commerce Commission. These reports are too elaborate to be presented here in full detail. The following condensation will show the more important elements in the income account.

UNION PACIFIC R. R. CO.
(YEAR ENDED DECEMBER 31, 1935)

Total Operating Revenue........................		$129,405,000
Maintenance of Ways & Structure....	$15,510,000	
Maintenance of Equipment..........	23,924,000	
Other Operating Expenses...........	53,968,000	93,402,000
Net Operating Revenue........................		36,003,000
Taxes............................	9,967,000	
Uncollectible Revenue...............	46,000	10,013,000
Railway Operating Income.......................		25,990,000
Equipment Rents (Net)............. Dr.	6,865,000	
Joint Facility Rents (Net)........... Dr.	510,000	Dr. 7,375,000
Net Railway Operating Income...................		18,615,000
Other Income:		
Interest and Dividends Received....	14,329,000	
Miscellaneous....................	924,000	15,253,000
Gross Income..................................		33,868,000
Miscellaneous Deductions.........................		813,000
Available for Fixed Charges......................		33,055,000

Fixed Charges:

Interest on Funded Debt..........	$14,438,000	
Other Charges....................	82,000	$14,520,000

Net Income...................................			18,535,000
Preferred Dividends.................	3,982,000		
Common Dividends.................	13,337,000		
Sinking Fund......................	10,000		17,329,000

			1,206,000
Surplus Additions—Sundry credits................		Cr.	106,000
Surplus Deductions:			
Loss on Property Retired..........	5,980,000		
Sundry Debits....................	285,000	Dr.	6,265,000

Net Decrease in Surplus for Year.................		4,953,000
Profit and Loss—Surplus Dec. 31, 1934 (per Balance		
Sheet)...................................		254,178,000
Profit and Loss—Surplus Dec. 31, 1935 (per Balance		
Sheet)...................................		249,225,000

The titles used above are those officially prescribed by the I. C. C. rules. Some of the more important items are frequently referred to under more popular names. For example:

Official Title	*Popular Title*
Total Operating Revenue	Gross Earnings or Gross Revenue
Railway Operating Income	Net After Taxes
Net Railway Operating Income	Net After Rents
Net Income	Balance for Dividends

The Joint Facility Rents represent amounts paid (dr.) or received (cr.) for the use of terminal facilities or trackage in common with some other carrier. Fixed Charges include not only the interest on bonds but also other interest payments and rentals for leased lines (operated as part of the system). Miscellaneous Deductions comprise taxes paid on non-railroad property, certain payments on guarantees, etc.

CHAPTER XXIX

CALCULATING EARNINGS

In studying a bond issue the most important figure is the number of times the total interest charges (and equivalent) are earned. Charges of the same nature as bond interest (such as other interest, rentals, amortization of bond discount) should be included therewith, and the number of times these "fixed charges" are covered should be computed. In dealing with the bonds of public utility and other holding companies, it is usually necessary to consider the subsidiaries' preferred dividends as fixed charges, for these may have to be paid before there is any income available for the parent company's bonds.

The coverage of interest or fixed charges is calculated, of course, by dividing these charges into the earnings available for them. Strictly speaking, income taxes should not first be deducted from earnings, but it is frequently more convenient to do so, and it gives a more conservative result. The earnings available for fixed charges may often be found most simply by working backwards from the balance available for dividends (net income) and adding the fixed charges thereto.

In the case of a senior bond issue, it may be useful to compute also the interest coverage without counting the charges on junior bonds. This is a supplementary figure, however, and must always be studied in conjunction with the total or "over-all" coverage. It is never correct to calculate the coverage on a *junior* issue alone, after deducting from income the requirements of the senior issues. This may give very misleading results, and in the case of a small junior issue may indicate that it is safer than the senior issues—which is manifestly absurd.

Where there is a preferred stock *not preceded by bonds* the earnings available for it may be shown either as the dollars earned per share or the number of times the dividends were covered. To find the earnings per share, simply divide the net income available for dividends by the number of shares. However, if there are bonds outstanding, the preferred dividend coverage should be calculated only in conjunction with the fixed charges or interest charges. In other words, you must calculate how many times the *total of fixed charges plus preferred dividends* was earned. It is common practice in these cases to calculate the preferred dividend separately, but that method is incorrect in the case of issues bought for investment and may give rise to seriously misleading results.

Common stock earnings are always shown as so much per share, and of course are computed after deducting preferred dividends at the full annual rate to which the issue is entitled, including the participating feature, if any. (Back dividends on a preferred stock are not deducted from current earnings in figuring the amount available for the common, but the existence of such accumulated dividends must of course be taken into account.)

EARNINGS CALCULATIONS 1935

	Example A (Amer. Gas & Elec. Co.)	Example B (Amer. Roll- ing Mill)	Example C (Union Pac. RR.)
Earnings Available for Fixed Charges..................	$24,159,761	$6,793,000	$33,055,000
Total Fixed Charges..........	13,603,319	2,483,000	14,520,000
Times Fixed Charges Earned...	1.78	2.73	2.28
Fixed Charges and Preferred Dividends...............	15,737,057	2,595,000	18,502,000
Times Preferred Dividends Earned "Over-All"........	1.54	2.61	1.79
Balance for Common Stock.....	8,422,704	4,198,000	14,553,000
Number of Shares Outstanding.	4,482,738	1,853,000	2,223,000
Earned per Common Share....	$1.88	$2.26	$6.55

Notes: Earnings for Fixed Charges are stated after deducting Federal Income Taxes and Minority Interest. This is the most conservative method.

The preferred dividends of American Rolling Mill Co. have been taken at the regular $6 rate, disregarding accumulations paid off in 1935, and those of the American Gas & Electric Co. at their regular annual rates. It is customary to calculate the earnings per share on the preferred stock, as follows:

	Example A	Example B	Example C
Balance for Preferred Dividends	$10,556,442	$4,310,000	$18,535,000
Number of Shares of Preferred Stock..................	355,623	19,324	995,000
Earned per Preferred share....	$29.68	$223.05	$18.62

Calculations of this sort must be viewed with reserve and used only in connection with the coverage of fixed charges and preferred dividends combined.

CHAPTER XXX

THE MAINTENANCE AND DEPRECIATION FACTOR

A thoroughgoing income account analysis takes a number of factors into consideration which we have not space to discuss. Something should be said, however, about maintenance and depreciation. By making excessive or insufficient allowances for these items the net earnings may readily be under- or over-stated. The maintenance figure is chiefly important in the railroad field. The usual maintenance figure (for way and equipment combined) is from 32% to 36% of gross. A wide departure from this range in either direction suggests that an adjustment of the reported earnings may be necessary, and in any event calls for further study.

In the case of the public utilities, the depreciation allowance is of major importance. While the depreciation charge is properly a certain percentage of the plant account, it usually is more convenient to study it in relation to the gross earnings. In most cases a suitable depreciation charge appears to be between 8% and 12% of gross. Some companies use a so-called Retirement Reserve in their statement to stockholders, which is almost always a considerably smaller figure than the regular "straight-line" depreciation charge which they take for income tax purposes. A discrepancy of this kind deserves careful attention. It may mean that, conservatively considered, the company's bonds are not nearly as safe as they look, or that its common stock is not really earning the amount reported to the shareholders.

Maintenance and depreciation allowances are not likely to be as important in the case of industrials as they are for railroads and utilities. There has been an absurd but growing tendency in recent years to write down the plant account heavily—even in some cases to $1—in order to "save" the annual depreciation charge and thus make the net earnings appear larger. This is merely fooling the stockholders; for regardless of book figures, the earnings should be charged with whatever wear and tear is actually suffered during the year, as measured by fair values.

In some very rare cases the depreciation charges are excessive, either because too high rates are used, or because the base values are far above replacement costs. In some special cases, also, if an investor can buy shares at current asset value only, thus paying nothing for the plant, he is justified in ignoring or substantially reducing the company's depreciation charges in making his private calculations. Similar considerations apply to the company's allowance for depletion.

The most recent data covering the amounts set aside by companies for depreciation are for the year 1933. For that year, 72 companies in extractive industries, such as mining, oil, etc., reported combined depreciation, depletion, and obsolescence charges amounting to 7.1% of the December 31, 1932, net property valuation. This may be regarded as a workable standard for comparison. In the nonextractive industries, such as manufacturing, etc., 80 concerns showed depreciation and obsolescence charges in 1933 averaging 4.5% of the net property value. Thirty-seven companies engaged in retail trade showed in 1933 depreciation and obsolescence charges averaging 5.2% of the net property value. As a general rule, about 5% of the net property value may be taken as an adequate annual depreciation charge for companies not in extractive industries.

CHAPTER XXXI

THE SAFETY OF INTEREST AND PREFERRED DIVIDENDS

In analyzing an investment grade bond, the coverage of Fixed Charges is the main criterion. In the case of a high grade preferred stock, the comparable test is the coverage of Fixed Charges plus Preferred Dividends. It is best to take a ten year average, but if a shorter period is used then completely abnormal years like 1931 and 1932 might justifiably be eliminated. The following minimum "over-all coverage" is recommended for investment bonds and preferred stocks. (These figures are higher than are ordinarily prescribed, but there is no harm in being over-conservative in choosing investments.)

MINIMUM AVERAGE EARNINGS COVERAGE

	BONDS Total Fixed Charges Earned	PREFERRED STOCKS Total Fixed Charges Plus Preferred Dividends Earned
Utilities..............	1¾ times	2 times
Railroads............	2 times	2½ times
Industrials...........	3 times	4 times

In an investment study of the income account, attention is given to the following additional factors among others: (1) the operating ratio—a figure obtained by dividing the operating expenses by the total revenue or sales. This is a measure of the operating efficiency of the company and also its ability to absorb reductions in volume or in selling price; (2) the ratio of fixed charges (or fixed charges and preferred dividends) to gross revenues; (3) the maintenance and depreciation charges; (4) the nature and amount of charges to surplus not included in the income account.

In studying these figures, comparisons should be made between various companies in the same field and also for the same company in successive years.

CHAPTER XXXII

TRENDS

A consistent change in some important factor in the income account over a period of time is known as a trend. The most important trends of course are those of interest and preferred dividends coverage, and of earnings available for the common stock, but these trends result in turn from favorable or unfavorable trends in the gross business, operating ratio, and fixed charges.

Obviously it is desirable that a company show a favorable trend in gross and net earnings. Securities of a company revealing a definitely unfavorable trend should not be bought for ordinary investment—even though the coverage may still be large—unless you are convinced that the trend will correct itself shortly. On the other hand, there is danger of attaching undue importance to a favorable trend, for this too may prove deceptive. In the case of investment issues it is well to require in every case that the *average* earnings show a satisfactory coverage for interest and preferred dividends.

In selecting common stocks it is proper to assign more weight to the indicated trend than in the purchase of investment issues, for a common stock can advance substantially in price if the trend continues. However, before purchasing a common stock because of its favorable trend it is well to ask two questions: (a) How certain am I that this favorable trend will continue, and (b) How large a price am I paying in advance for the expected continuance of the trend?

CHAPTER XXXIII

COMMON STOCK PRICES AND VALUES

Broadly speaking, the price of common stocks is governed by the prospective earnings. These prospective earnings are, of course, a matter of estimate or foresight; and the action of the stock market on this point is usually controlled by the indicated trend. The trend is gauged in turn from the past record and current data, although at times the expectation of some quite new development will pay a determining part.

The price of common stocks will depend, therefore, not so much on past or current earnings in themselves as upon what the security buying public thinks the future earnings will be. (There are also important influences of a general or technical nature affecting stock prices—such as credit, political, and psychological conditions—which may not be closely related to any estimate of future earnings; but such influences will either eventually reflect themselves in the earnings or else prove to be quite temporary.)

In the ordinary case the price of a common stock is the resultant of the many estimates of what the earnings are going to be in the next six months, in the next year, or even further in the future. Some of these estimates may be entirely incorrect and some may be exceedingly accurate; but the buying and selling by the many people who make these various estimates is what mainly determines the present price of a stock.

The accepted idea that a common stock should sell at a certain ratio to its current earnings must be considered more the result of practical necessity than of logic. The market takes the trend or future prospects into account by varying this ratio for different types of companies. Common stocks of enterprises with only slight possibilities of increasing profits ordinarily sell at a rather low price-earning ratio (less than 15 times their current earnings); and the common stocks of companies with good prospects of increasing the earnings usually sell at high price-earnings ratio (over 15 times the current earnings). Thus, two common stocks may show the same current earnings per share, may be paying the same dividend rate, and be in equally good financial condition. Yet stock ABC may be selling at twice the price of stock XYZ simply because security buyers believe that stock ABC is going to earn a good deal more than XYZ next year and the years after.

When neither boom nor deep depression is affecting the market, the judgment of the public on individual issues, as indicated by market prices, is usually quite good. If the market price of some issue appears out of line with the facts and figures available, it will often be found later that the price is discounting future developments not then apparent on the surface. There is, however, a frequent tendency on the part of the stock market to exaggerate the significance of changes in earnings both in a favorable and unfavorable direction. This is manifest in the market as a whole in periods of both boom and depression, and it is also evidenced in the case of individual companies at other times.

At bottom the ability to buy securities—particularly common stocks—successfully is the ability to look ahead accurately. Looking backward, however carefully, will not suffice, and may do more harm than good. Common stock selection is a difficult art—naturally, since it offers large rewards for success. It requires a skillful mental balance between the facts of the past and the possibilities of the future.

CHAPTER XXXIV

CONCLUSION

In the preceding chapters you have seen the various factors to be considered in reading financial statements. By an examination of the statements it is possible to form an opinion as to the present position and potentialities of the company. The asset value, the earning power of the company, the financial position as compared with other companies in the same industry, the trend of earnings, and the ability of the management to meet constantly changing conditions—all of these factors have an important bearing on the value of the company's securities.

However, there are other factors outside the control of the company that are perhaps equally important in their influence on the value of its securities. The outlook for the industry, general business and security-market conditions, periods of inflation or depression, artificial market influences, the popular favor of the type of security—these factors cannot be measured in terms of exact ratios and margins of safety. They can only be judged by a general knowledge gained by constant contact with financial and business news.

Knowledge of securities is becoming more and more widespread among the general public. While this development gives an increasingly wide field for security salesmen and customers' men, it demands more and more accurate knowledge on their part.

The investor who buys securities when the market price looks cheap on the basis of the company's statements, and sells them when they look high on this same basis, probably will not make spectacular profits. But on the other hand, he will probably avoid equally spectacular and more frequent losses. He should have a better than average chance of obtaining satisfactory results. And this is the chief objective of intelligent investing.

PART II

ANALYZING A BALANCE SHEET AND INCOME ACCOUNT BY THE RATIO METHOD

ANALYZING A BALANCE SHEET AND INCOME ACCOUNT BY THE RATIO METHOD

A number of the ratios used in the analysis of an industrial company's income account and balance sheet are presented herewith by the use of a single example —namely the financial statements of the Bethlehem Steel Corporation for 1928. Various items in the Balance Sheet and Income Account are numbered. This will facilitate the explanation as to the method of computing ratios. For example, margin of profit, the first ratio computed in this study, is operating income divided by sales. On the Income Account operating income is item No. 4 and sales is item No. 1. The method of computing margin of profit is expressed as (4) ÷ (1) or in actual amounts $27,271,108 ÷ $294,778,287 = 9.2%.

BETHLEHEM STEEL CORPORATION
INCOME ACCOUNT YEAR ENDED DECEMBER 31, 1928

(1) Sales...	$294,778,287
(2) Deduct-Manufacturing cost, administrative, selling and general expense and taxes...............	253,848,844
	40,929,443
(3) Provision for depletion, depreciation and obsolescence................................	13,658,335

(4) Operating Income................................ $ 27,271,108
    Add—interest, dividends and other miscellaneous income.. 2,591,693

(5) Total Income................................... 29,862,801
(6) Deduct-Interest charges......................... 11,276,879

(7) Net Income.................................... 18,585,922
(8) Deduct-Dividends on Preferred Stock............ 6,842,500

(9) Net for Common Stock.......................... 11,743,422
    Deduct-Dividends on Common Stock.......... 1,800,000

(10) Transferred to Surplus......................... $ 9,943,422

CONSOLIDATED BALANCE SHEET
BETHLEHEM STEEL CORPORATION
December 31, 1928

ASSETS

Current Assets:

(11) Cash............................	$28,470,936	
(12) U. S. Government securities	27,247,838	
Sundry marketable securities........	1,980,000	
Preferred stock held for employees less payments on account.............	7,742,698	
(13) Accounts and notes receivable.......	41,951,684	
(14) Inventories.......................	61,539,137	
(15) Total Current Assets........................		$168,932,293
Reserve Fund Assets..........................		6,917,227
Sundry securities, and real estate installment contracts and mortgages........................		3,837,820
Funds in hands of Trustees....................		691,311
Investments in and advances to affiliated companies.		8,654,700
(16) Property account.................	$654,731,533	
(17) Less reserve for depreciation and depletion......................	200,408,672	
(18) Property account (net)........................		454,322,855
Total Assets.................................		$643,356,206

LIABILITIES

Current Liabilities:

Accounts payable and accrued liabilities......................	25,227,323	
Bond Interest accrued..............	2,998,122	
Preferred stock dividend payable January 2, and April 1, 1929......	3,447,500	
Common stock dividend payable May 15, 1929..................	1,800,000	
(19) Total Current Liabilities....................		33,472,945

(20)	Funded debt...............................		$199,421,172
(21)	Cambria Iron Company stock (annual rental of 4% payable)...............................		8,465,625
	Capital Stock, Surplus and Reserves:		
(22)	7% Cumulative Pfd. Stock, $100 par value........................	100,000,000	
(23)	Common Stock, $100 par value $180,000,000		
(24)	Surplus............. 114,922,652		
	Contingent reserve.... 2,138,990		
	Insurance reserve..... 4,934,822	301,996,464	401,996,464
	Total Liabilities...........................		$643,356,206

(a) *Margin of Profit*

Operating income divided by Sales.

Formula: (4) ÷ (1)

In this case: $27,271,108 ÷ $294,778,287 = 9.2%

This ratio is used in determining the operating efficiency of the company. This ratio of 9.2 % means that for every dollar of sales, the company has 9.2 cents left after paying all the costs of operations. From this 9.2 cents (plus "other income") must be paid bond interest, preferred and common dividends and (formerly) an amount set aside for surplus.

(b) *Earnings on Invested Capital*

Total income available for interest charges divided by the sum of the Bonds, Preferred Stock, Common Stock and earned surplus.

Formula: 5 ÷ (20 plus 21 plus 22 plus 23 plus 24)

In this case: $29,862,801 ÷ $602,809,449 = 4.95%

This means that in 1928 the company earned 4.95% on the money invested in the business. The percentage earned on the invested capital varies with the industry. The average for 25 steel companies for that year was slightly over 6%.

(c) *Times Interest Charges Earned*

Total income divided by interest charges.

Formula: (5) ÷ (6)

In this case: $29,862,801 ÷ $11,276,879 = 2.65

It is generally conceded that an industrial company

should earn its total interest charges at least 2½ times on the average. We prefer a minimum of three times for a high grade industrial bond.

(d) *Times Interest Charges and Preferred Dividend Earned*
Total Income divided by the sum of interest charges and preferred dividends.
Formula: 5 ÷ (6 plus 8)
In this case: $29,862,801 ÷ ($11,276,879 plus $6,842,-500) = 1.65 times
We believe that interest charges plus preferred dividends should be earned fully four times on the average to warrant purchase of an industrial preferred stock on a straight investment basis.

(e) *Earnings per Share on the Common Stock*
Net Income available for Common Stock divided by the number of shares of Common Stock outstanding.
Formula: (9) ÷ (23) (expressed in shares)
In this case: $11,743,422 ÷ 1,800,000 = $6.52 per share

(f) *Depreciation as a Percentage of Cost of Plant*
Depreciation divided by cost of Plant.
Formula: (3) ÷ (16)
In this case: $13,658,355 ÷ $654,731,533 = 2.09%
This means that the average life of all the items in the property account (including real estate which lasts forever) is taken at 50 years. The ratio of 2.09% is somewhat lower than the average of 2.7% for some 13 steel companies in 1928.
Sometimes for comparative purposes it is necessary to take the ratio of annual depreciation to *net* plant account.
Formula: (3) ÷ (18)
In this case: $13,658,355 ÷ $454,322,855 = 3.01%

(g) *Depreciation as a Percentage of Sales or Gross Revenues*
This ratio is also useful at times in making comparisons.
Formula: (3) ÷ (1)
In this case: $13,658,355 ÷ $294,778,287 = 4.63%

(h) *Net Income Transferred to Surplus as a Percentage of Net Income Available for Dividends*

Amount transferred to surplus divided by net income available for dividends.

Formula: (10) ÷ (7)

In this case: $9,943,422 ÷ $18,585,922 = 53.5%

Calculations of this kind should be made over a period of years, and would then show if the company has been pursuing a conservative dividend policy. It has been generally considered that an industrial company should transfer to surplus (i.e., retain in the business) about 30% or 40% of the amount available for dividends.

Because of the new Undistributed Profits Tax, amounts retained in the business are now likely to be represented by additional share capital. For purposes of this calculation such stock capital may be considered as the equivalent of an addition to surplus.

(i) *Inventory Turnover*

Sales divided by inventory.

Formula: (1) ÷ (14)

In this case: $294,778,287 ÷ $61,539,137 = 4.7 times a year*

The Company "turns its inventory over" 4.7 times a year. This is considered a good ratio. Inventory turnover is important because the more times a year a company can turn its inventory, the less capital is invested in inventory, and there is less chance of loss through obsolete material, etc.

(j) *Number of Days Average Account Receivable Is Outstanding*

Accounts and Notes Receivable divided by net daily sales.

* The real or physical turnover is found by dividing inventory, which is carried at cost, into "cost of sales." Formula: (2) ÷ (14). In this case the turnover would be 4.15 times.

Formula $(13) \div \dfrac{(1)}{365}$

In this case $\$41,951,654 \div \dfrac{\$294,778,287}{365} = 52$ days

The company that year had its average account receivable outstanding for a period of 52 days. This ratio is used in determining the credit policy of the company.

(k) *Capitalization Ratios*

Bond Capitalization

Amount of bonds outstanding divided by the sum of the Bonds, Preferred stock, Common stock and Surplus.

Formula: (20 plus 21) $\div$ (20 plus 21 plus 22 plus 23 plus 24)

In this case: $\$207,886,797 \div \$602,809,449 = 34.4\%$

Cambria Iron Stock is included in the bonds because payment of the 4% dividend on the stock is guaranteed in connection with the leasing of the properties.

Preferred Stock Capitalization

Preferred Stock divided by the sum of the Bonds, Preferred stock, Common stock and Surplus.

Formula: 22 $\div$ (20 plus 21 plus 22 plus 23 plus 24)

In this case: $\$100,000,000 \div \$602,809,449 = 16.6\%$

Common Stock and Surplus Capitalization

The sum of Common stock and the Surplus divided by the sum of Bonds, Preferred stock, Common stock and Surplus.

Formula: (23 plus 24) $\div$ (20 plus 21 plus 22 plus 23 plus 24)

In this case: $\$294,922,652 \div \$602,809,449 = 49.0\%$

To summarize, the Company is capitalized as follows: 34.4% in Bonds, 16.6% in Preferred stock and 49.0% in Common stock. The ordinary industrial company should not have much more than 25% or

30% of its total capitalization in bonds. About one-half of the total capitalization should be represented by Common stock and Surplus.

The same calculation may usefully be made by taking Preferred and Common stock at current market prices, instead of using the book values including surplus. This calculation is known as the stock value ratio. The formula for the stock value ratio for bonds is: Total market value of Preferred and Common stocks ÷ total par value of Bonds. The formula for stock value ratio for Preferred stock is: Total market value of Common stock ÷ sum of total par value of Bonds plus total market value of Preferred stocks.

(1) *Current Ratio*

Current Assets divided by Current Liabilities.

Formula: $(15) \div (19)$

In this case: $168,932,293 ÷ $33,472,945 = 5.04 to 1

In other words the Company has $5.04 in Current Assets (assets which in the normal course of business will have been turned into cash at the expiration of one year) for each dollar in current liabilities (liabilities which in the normal course of business will have to be paid off within a year). The ratio of 5.04 to 1 is satisfactory for a steel company. The current ratio varies widely among the various industries, but 2 to 1 is considered a minimum. (See table in Chapter XIV.)

(m) *Quick Assets Ratio*

Current Assets less Inventory divided by Current Liabilities.

Formula: $(15 - 14) \div (19)$

In this case: $107,393,156 ÷ $33,472,945 = 3.2 to 1

To put it another way the Company has $3.20 in quick assets for each dollar in current liabilities. This is a good ratio. About 1 to 1 is considered fair.

(n) *Book Value of Common Stock*

The sum of Common Stock and Surplus divided by the number of shares of Common Stock outstanding.

Formula: (23 plus 24) ÷ 23 (expressed in shares)

In this case: $294,922,652 ÷ 1,800,000 = $164 per share

It is customary to exclude intangible assets (good will, patents, etc.) from book value—i.e., they would be deducted from the sum of common stock and surplus.

The book value of a common stock is usually not important, but it may be of interest where the book value is either much larger or much smaller than the market price.*

(o) *Price-Earnings Ratio or Market Ratio*

Selling price of the stock divided by the earnings per share. On May 15, 1929, Bethlehem Steel Common closed at 105⅝. 105⅝ ÷ $6.52 = 16.2 which means that the stock was selling at 16.2 times 1928 earnings. This ratio is used in determining whether a stock is relatively high or low priced, and as a starting point in comparative analysis.

*Note: See also Chapter XXIV—Net Current Asset Value.

PART III

DEFINITIONS OF FINANCIAL TERMS AND PHRASES

DEFINITIONS OF FINANCIAL TERMS
AND PHRASES

Acceleration Clause. Provision in a bond indenture whereby the principal may be declared due in advance of maturity, because of default in payment of interest or some other "event of default."

Accruals. Expenses charged against current operations but not requiring cash payment therefor until some future date. Thus, bond interest may be accrued on the corporation's books each month, although it usually is paid only at six-month intervals. Accruals may also refer to credit items, such as interest accrued on securities held.

Accumulative (Dividends). Same as Cumulative.

Adjustment Bonds. See Income Bonds.

"After Acquired Property" Clause. A provision in a mortgage indenture which places property subsequently acquired by the issuing company under the lien of the mortgage.

Amortization. The process of gradually extinguishing a liability, deferred charge, or capital expenditure over a period of time. Thus, (a) a mortgage is amortized by periodically paying off part of the face amount; (b) bond discount is amortized by periodically charging the earnings of each year during which the bonds are outstanding with their proper share of the total discount; (c) fixed assets are amortized by charges for depreciation, depletion and obsolescence.

Arbitrage. Simultaneous completion of purchase and sale of securities (or commodities) at a profit-yielding price spread, made possible by (1) existence of trading in such security or commodity in more than one market place; or (2) by existence of two separate securities with established terms of exchange from one to the other. Example of (1): Simultaneous sale in the London market and purchase in New York of United States Steel at a spread sufficient to provide expenses plus a profit; example of (2): Simultaneous sale in the same market place of a common stock and the purchase of a bond or preferred stock currently convertible at a definite ratio into such stock, or of "rights" entitling the owner upon payment of a fixed amount of cash to acquire such stock, the spread in prices being sufficient to provide expenses plus a profit.

Articles of Association. A document similar to a charter or certificate of incorporation setting forth the terms under which an enterprise is authorized by the state to do business.

Asset Value. The same as definition (b) of Book Value.

Assets. The valuable resources, or properties and property rights, owned by a corporation. See Capital Assets, Current Assets, Deferred Assets, Intangible Assets, and Tangible Assets.

Audit. An examination of the financial status and operations of an enterprise, based mostly on the books of account, and undertaken to secure information for or to check the accuracy of the enterprise's Balance Sheet, Income Statement and/or Surplus Statement. See also Certified Report.

Balance Sheet. A report of the financial status of an enterprise on a specific date. It lists in one column all the assets owned and their values and in another column the claims of creditors and the equity of the owners. The two columns are always equal in total amount.

Bankers' Shares. A name given to certificates, generally issued by banks, each representing a fractional part of the share of some deposited stock. The usual purpose is to create a stock issue selling at a much lower price than the original shares. Also called Trustee Shares.

Basis. In the case of bonds, either the yield to maturity at a given price, as shown by the Bond Tables, or the price corresponding to a given yield to maturity.

Bills Payable. Technically, unconditional orders in writing upon the enterprise by another enterprise or person for the payment of a sum of money. In practice they usually represent bank loans payable.

Blue Chip Issues. A colloquial term applied to stocks which are of accepted investment merit, but with abnormally high ratio of price to current earnings and dividends, and are popular market leaders.

"Blue Sky" Flotations. Originally applied to promotions of companies whose securities have no value. So named, because the purchaser receives no more than "blue sky" for his money. State and Federal laws to prevent such flotations are now in force. Registration of securities under such laws is now called "blue-skying."

Bond. A certificate of debt which (a) represents a part of a loan to a business corporation or governmentality, (b) bears interest, and (c) matures on a stated future date. Infrequently a bond issue may fail to possess one of these characteristics. Short term bonds (generally running for five years or less from date of issuance) are often called Notes.

Bond Discount. In financial statements, represents the excess of the face value of a bond issue over the net amount received therefor by the issuing corporation. This discount usually is amortized over the life of the bonds. In popular investment parlance, represents the excess of the face value of a bond over its current market price. A bond "selling at a discount" is one selling at a price less than 100, or par. Conversely, a bond "selling at a premium" is at a price above par.

Bonds, Straight. Bonds conforming to the standard pattern;

i.e., (a) unqualified right to repayment of a fixed principal amount on a fixed date, (b) unqualified right to fixed interest payment on fixed dates, (c) no further interest in assets or profits, and no voice in the management.

Bonds, Underlying. Bonds which have precedence over some other bond or bonds. They usually hold a first mortgage on property of a corporation which is also pledged under a junior General Mortgage.

Book Value. (a) of an asset: The value at which it is carried on the company's books. (b) of a stock or bond issue: The value of the assets available for that issue, as stated on the books, after deducting all prior liabilities. It is generally stated at so much per share or so much per $1,000 bond. The accepted practice excludes intangibles in computing book value, which is thus the same as "tangible asset value."

Break-Up Value. In the case of an investment trust or a holding company issue, the value of the assets available for the issue, taking all marketable securities at their market price.

Business Man's Investment. An investment in which a certain amount of risk is recognized but is thought to be offset either by the chance of increased principal value or by a high income return. (In our view, the second consideration is generally unsound.) This term is based on the thought that a business man is both financially able to assume some risk and capable of following his investments intelligently.

Callable Feature. A provision of a bond issue by which it may be retired in advance of maturity at the option of the company—not the holder. The feature may provide for various prices at various times. Also applies to preferred stock.

Capital (of a business). (a) In the narrower sense, the dollar value assigned in the balance sheet to the various stock issues; (b) in a broader sense the investment represented by the stock issues and the surplus, and (c) in a still broader sense the same as the foregoing, but adding thereto all long term obligations. (See capitalization.)

Capital Assets or Fixed Assets. Assets of a relatively permanent nature which are held for use or income rather than for sale or direct conversion into salable goods or cash. The chief capital assets are real estate, buildings and equipment, often referred to together as "plant account" or "property account." Intangible assets, such as good-will, patents, etc., are also capital assets.

Capital Expenditures. Expenditures or outlays of cash or its equivalent which are undertaken to increase or improve capital assets. Cf. Revenue Expenditures.

Capitalization. The aggregate of the various securities issued by a corporation including bonds, preferred stock, and common stock. (It is sometimes a question of judgment whether a short-term obligation should be considered part of the capitalization or as a non-capital current liability. If it falls due within a year, it is usually considered to be a current liability.)

Capital Structure. The division of the capitalization as between bonds, preferred stock, and common stock. Where common stock represents all or nearly all of the capitalization, the structure may be called "conservative"; where common stock represents a small percentage of the total, the structure is called "speculative."

Capitalizing Expenditures. Certain kinds of expenditures may at the option of the company be treated either as a current expense or a capital expense. In the latter case the expenditure appears on the balance sheet as an asset, which is generally written off gradually over a period of years. Examples of such expenditures: Intangible drilling costs (of oil concerns); development expense (in mines, and by manufacturing companies); organization expense; expense of floating bond or stock issues, etc.

Capitalizing Fixed Charges. Computing the principal amount of a debt which would carry the fixed charges in question. Method: Divide the fixed charges by the assumed interest rate. Example: Fixed charges of $100,000, capitalized at 4%, yield a principal value of

$$\frac{\$100,000}{.04} = \$2,500,000.$$

Capital Surplus. See Surplus.

Cash Asset Value. The value of the cash assets (cash and cash equivalents) alone applicable to a given security issue, after deducting all prior liabilities. Ordinarily stated at so much per share or per $1,000 bond. The Cash Asset Value of a stock is sometimes stated without deducting liabilities from the cash assets. This should be termed the "gross cash asset value," and it is a useful calculation only when the other assets exceed all the prior liabilities.

Cash Equivalents. Assets held in place of cash and convertible into cash within a short time. Examples: Time deposits, U. S. Government bonds and other marketable securities.

Certificate of Deposit. (a) A receipt for a security deposited with a protective committee or for some purpose such as a reorganization plan. These certificates of deposit, known as "c/d"s are generally transferable and are dealt in as securities. (b) The same as a time deposit.

Certified Report. A corporate report (Balance Sheet, Income Statement and/or Surplus Statement), the correctness of which is attested to by a certified public accountant as the result of an independent audit. It always is advisable to study carefully the accountant's certificate appended to the report, since audits vary widely as to their scope, and a given audit may be subject to important limitations and reservations.

Charter. The certificate of incorporation or franchise received from the state, legally authorizing the corporation to carry on business as set forth under the grant of powers in the charter.

Civil Loans. Loans contracted by a government agency—national, state or municipal.

Class "A" Stock. A name given to a stock issue to distinguish it from some other stock issue of the same company, generally called Class "B" or merely common. The difference may lie in voting rights, dividend or asset preferences, or other special dividend provisions. If there is a preference, it is generally held by the Class "A" shares, but other advantages may go either to the Class "A" issue or to the other common stock issue.

Collateral-Trust Bonds. Bonds secured by other securities (either stocks or bonds) deposited with a trustee. The real investment merit of these bonds depends upon either or both of (1) the financial responsibility of the company issuing them, and (2) the value of the deposited securities.

Consolidation. A combination of two or more companies into one, to form a new company. See Merger.

Consolidated Statement. A corporate report (Balance Sheet, Income Statement and/or Surplus Statement) that combines the separate statements of the corporation and its subsidiaries. Such consolidated reports eliminate all intercompany accounts, and show the entire group of companies as if it were a single enterprise.

Contingent Liabilities. Liabilities indefinite as to either their amount or their occurrence. Examples: amounts involved in law suits or tax claims; liabilities under a guarantee.

Contingency Reserves. Reserves set up out of earnings or surplus to indicate a possible future loss or claim against the corporation, the likelihood of which is open to considerable question (e.g., possible future decline in the market value of inventories or marketable securities owned). In most cases they may be regarded as part of the surplus, but occasionally indicate *probable* as well as merely possible losses or claims.

Controlled Company. A company whose policies are controlled by another through ownership of 51% or more of its voting stock.

Conversion Parity or Conversion Level. That price of the common stock which is equivalent to a given quotation for a convertible issue, or vice versa. For example, if a preferred stock is convertible into three shares of common and sells at 90, the conversion parity for the common would be 30. If the common is selling at 25, the conversion parity for the preferred would be 75. This may also be called the *conversion value* of the preferred stock.

Conversion Price. That price of the common stock equivalent to a price of 100 for a convertible bond or a convertible preferred stock of $100 par value. For example, if a $1,000 bond is convertible into 40 shares of common stock, the conversion price of the common is $25 a share.

Conversion Privilege. See Convertible Issues.

Convertible Bonds. Bonds which are convertible into other securities at a prescribed price or ratio *at the option of the holder*. Usually convertible into the common stock of the corporation but sometimes convertible into preferred stock, or even into other bonds. The holder is in the position of a creditor of the corporation with the privilege of additional profits if the enterprise is successful.

Convertible Issues. Securities which may be exchanged for other securities in accordance with provisions of the indenture (bonds), or the charter or by-laws (stock).

Credit. See Debit & Credit.

Cumulative Deductions Method. A method of computing bond interest coverage which takes into account only the interest on bonds of prior or equal rank to the issue being considered. Interest on bonds of junior rank is ignored by this method. This method should be used, if at all, only as a secondary test, supplementing the "over-all" method. See Over-All Method.

Cumulative Preferred Stock. Preferred stock entitled to dividends at a fixed rate and entitled to receive all such dividends not paid in previous years before the common stock can receive any payment. Some issues are cumulative only to the extent that dividends have been earned but unpaid in any year. (Suggested title for these: earned-cumulative issues.)

Cumulative Voting. An arrangement whereby each share of

stock may cast as many votes for one director as there are directors to be elected. Its effect is to permit a substantial minority to elect one or more directors. Mandatory in some states (e.g., Pennsylvania, Michigan) and specified by the by-laws of some corporations in other states.

Current Assets. Assets which either are cash or can be readily turned into cash or will be converted into cash fairly rapidly in the normal course of business. Include cash, cash equivalents, receivables due within one year and inventories. (Slow-moving inventory should properly be excluded from current assets, but it is not customary to do so.)

Current Asset Value. The value of the current assets alone applicable to a given security, after deducting all prior liabilities. Ordinarily stated as so much per share or so much per $1,000 bond.

Current Liabilities. Recognized claims against the enterprise which are considered to be payable within one year.

Debentures. Obligations of a corporation secured only by the general credit of the corporation. Have no direct lien on specific property of the corporation. (Sometimes applied, with no special meaning, to a preferred stock issue.)

Debit & Credit. Bookkeeping terms to describe types of accounts and entries to accounts. Entries to the left side of an account are called debits, and accounts which normally have left-side balances (asset accounts and expense accounts) are called debit accounts. One debits an account to record an increase in an asset, a decrease in a liability, or an expense. Entries to the right side of accounts are called credits, and accounts with right-side balances (liability accounts, owners' equities accounts, and revenue or profit accounts) are called credit accounts. One credits an account to record a decrease in an asset, an increase in a liability, or a revenue or profit.

Deed of Trust. See Indenture.

Deferred Assets, or Deferred Charges. Bookkeeping assets representing certain kinds of outlays which will eventually be treated as expenses. They are not immediately charged to any expense account because they are more properly chargeable against future years' operations. Include unamortized bond discount, organization expense, development expense, and prepaid advertising, insurance, and rent. These latter prepaid expenses are sometimes called prepaid assets.

Deferred Maintenance. The amount of repairs that should have been made to keep plant in good running condition, but that have been put off to some future time. This measure of equipment neglect does not appear in the corporate reports, although its existence frequently is suggested by maintenance expenditures drastically lower than those of earlier years. This is most readily noticeable in the income accounts of railroads.

Deficit. When appearing in the balance sheet, represents the amount by which assets fall short of equalling the sum of liabilities (creditors' claims) and capital stock. When appearing in the income statement, usually represents the amount by which revenues fell short of equalling expenses and charges. An "operating deficit" means a loss *before* deducting fixed charges. "Deficit after dividends" is self-explanatory.

Depletion. The reduction in the value of a wasting asset due to the removal of part of that asset, e.g., through mining ore reserves or cutting timber.

Depletion Reserve. The valuation reserve reflecting the total depletion to date of the assets to which it pertains (usually mineral or timber resources). Deduction of this reserve from the corresponding balance sheet asset indicates the corporation's valuation of what remains of the asset, i.e., its net value.

Depreciation. The loss in value of a capital asset, due to wear and tear that cannot be compensated for by ordinary repairs, or to allowance for the asset's becoming obsolete before it wears out. The purpose of the bookkeeping charge for depreciation is to write off the original cost of an asset by equitably distributed charges against operations over its entire useful life. (When in any year more is charged on the books for depreciation than is reinvested in plant, the excess may be called "unexpended depreciation.")

Development Expense. (a) The cost of developing manufacturing or other processes or products to make them commercially usable. New enterprises frequently treat such items as deferred assets; established and successful enterprises more frequently treat them as current expense. (b) The cost of opening up a mining property—in most cases treated as a deferred asset.

Depreciation Reserve. The valuation reserve reflecting the total book depreciation to date—and therefore indicating the expired portion of the useful life—of the assets to which it pertains. A depreciation reserve of $200,000 against a $1,000,000 asset indicates, not that the asset's present resale value is $800,000, but merely that about 20% of the asset's useful life is believed to have expired.

Dilution. From the standpoint of a convertible issue, an increase in the number of common shares without a corresponding increase in the company's assets. Most convertible issues are protected against this contingency by an "anti-dilution clause," which reduces the conversion price in the event of dilution.

Diversification. Spreading the risk of investment by dividing the funds to be invested among a number of issues. An investment fund may diversify among different industries, or—less effectively—among different companies in the same industry; or geographically.

Dividend Coverage. The number of times a dividend has been earned in a given period. Preferred dividend coverage should properly be stated only as the number of times the combined fixed charges and preferred dividends have been earned. Common dividend coverage is stated separately, but the figure must be viewed in the light of the senior obligations.

Dividend Yield. A percentage figure, found by dividing the dividend rate in dollars by the market price in dollars. Example: If a stock paying $4 annually sells at $80, the dividend yield is $\frac{4}{80} = 5.00\%$.

Dividend Scrip. (a) Certificates issued as a scrip dividend. (See Scrip Dividend.) (b) Fractional shares of stock, received as a stock dividend. These fractional shares usually are not entitled to dividends or voting power until combined into full shares.

Divisional Liens. A term usually applied to bonds secured by a mortgage on a section of minor length of a railroad system. If the mileage covered by the lien is a valuable part of the system, the specific security is good. If the mileage covered by the lien is of small value to the system the specific security is poor.

Earned Surplus. See Surplus.

Earning Power. Properly, a rate of earnings which is considered as "normal," or reasonably probable, for the company or particular security. It should be based both upon the past record, and upon a reasonable assurance that the future will not be vastly different from the past. Hence companies with highly variable records or especially uncertain futures may not logically be thought of as having a well defined earning power. However, the term is often loosely used to refer to the average earnings over any given period, or even to the *current* earnings rate.

Earnings Yield. The ratio of the market price to the annual earnings. Example: A stock earning $6 annually and selling at 50, shows an earnings yield of 12%. See also Price-Earnings Ratio.

Earnings Rate. The annual earnings stated as so much per share, or (less frequently) as a percentage of the par value.

Earnings Ratio. (See Price-Earnings Ratio.) The relationship between the annual earnings and the market price, in which the price is expressed as a multiple of the earnings. In the example under "earnings yield," the price-earnings ratio would be stated as 8 1/3 to 1.

Effective Debt. The total debt of a company, including the principal value of annual lease or other payments which are equivalent to interest charges. (Such may not appear as part of the funded debt.) The effective debt may be calculated by capitalizing fixed charges (see definition) at an appropriate rate. Where long-term bond issues carry an abnormally high or an abnormally low coupon rate, the effective debt may be thought of as higher or lower than the face value.

Effective Par. In the case of preferred stocks, the par value which would ordinarily correspond to a given rate of dividend. Found by capitalizing the dividend in dollars at an appropriate rate, say 6%. Example: The effective par of a \$2.40 preferred stock would be $\frac{2.40}{.06} = 40$. Useful when dealing with no-par preferred issues or those having a par out of line with the dividend rate.

Equipment Obligations or Equipment Trust Certificates. Bonds, usually maturing serially, secured by a lien on the rolling stock of a railroad. There are two methods generally used to protect the creditor: (1) the Philadelphia Plan—now almost universal (title to equipment rests in hands of trustee until all certificates have been paid off, at which time title is transferred to the corporation); (2) the New York Plan (a conditional bill of sale is given to the corporation which issues the certificates; after the certificates have been paid off the corporation receives unqualified title).

Equipment Rentals. Sums paid by one railroad, generally to another railroad, for the use of rolling stock. These payments are on a per diem (per day) basis, in accordance with a standard schedule. The amounts paid or received appear in the railroad income statement immediately after the tax item.

Equipment Trust. An arrangement relating to the ownership or control of equipment (usually rolling stock of railroads) by a trustee, under which equipment trust certificates or bonds are issued. Often used to mean equipment trust certificates.

Equity. The interest of the stockholders in a company, as measured by the capital and surplus. Also the protection afforded a senior issue by reason of the existence of a junior investment.

Equity Securities. (a) Any stock issue, whether preferred or common. (b) More specifically, a common stock or any issue equivalent thereto through having a virtually unlimited interest in the assets and earnings of the company (after prior claims, if any).

Equity, Trading on the. When a business man borrows money for his business, to supplement his owned capital, he is said to be "trading on the equity." The underlying idea is that more profit can be made on the borrowed capital than the interest paid thereon. The phrase is sometimes used to mean specifically the extreme case where most of the capital is borrowed and only a small amount is owned.

Expenditures vs. Expenses. Expenditures are outlays of cash or the equivalent; frequently they involve no concurrent charge against operations or earnings (e.g., Capital Expenditures). Expenses are costs, i.e., charges against current operations or earnings; frequently they involve no concurrent cash expenditure (e.g., Accruals, Depreciation).

Factor of Safety. A method of stating fixed charge coverage, as the percentage of the balance after fixed charges to the fixed charges. Example: Earnings available for interest, $175,000; interest charge, $100,000. Factor of safety equals $\dfrac{175,000 - 100,000}{100,000} = 75\%$. Factor of safety equals (Interest Coverage $-$ 1) $\times$ 100%. (This term is becoming obsolete.)

Fiscal Year. The 12-month period selected by a corporation as the basis for computing and reporting profits. Usually coincides with the calendar year (i.e., ends December 31) but often differs from it. Many merchandising companies' fiscal years end January 31, to facilitate inventory taking after the close of the most active season, while some meat packers' fiscal years end October 31, for the same reason.

Fixed Assets. See Capital Assets.

Fixed Charges. Interest charges and other deductions equivalent thereto. These include rentals, guaranteed dividends, subsidiary preferred dividends ranking ahead of parent company charges and amortization of bond discount (the annual allowance to write off discount on bonds sold). Ordinarily building rents are not considered as fixed charges, but are included in operating expenses.

Floating Assets. Same as current assets.

Flush Production. In the oil industry, the large production yielded by new oil wells during the first period of their life. This lasts a short time and is succeeded by a "settled production" at a much smaller rate. In analysis it is important not to consider the earnings from flush production as permanent.

Foreclosure. The legal process of enforcing payment of a debt secured by a mortgage, by taking the properties which it covers and selling them. This may be done when the principal or interest on the mortgage is not paid.

Funded Debt. Debt represented by securities, i.e., by formal written agreements evidencing the borrower's obligation to pay a specified amount at a specified time and place, with interest at a specified rate. Includes bonds, debentures, and notes, but does not include bank loans.

Going Concern Value. The value of an enterprise considered as an operating business, and therefore based on its earning power and prospects rather than on liquidation of its assets.

Gold Clause. A clause in virtually all bonds issued for many years prior to 1933, under which payment was promised in gold dollars of the same weight and fineness as existed when the debt was contracted. No longer legal since 1933.

Good-Will. Intangible Asset purporting to reflect the capitalization of excess future profits expected to accrue as a result of some special intangible advantage held, such as good name, reputation, strategic location, or special connections. In practice, the amount at which good-will is carried on the balance sheet is rarely an accurate measure of its true value.

Gross Income. Sometimes used as the equivalent of Gross Sales. More often represents an intermediate figure between Gross Sales and Net Income.

Gross Revenues or Gross Sales. Total business done, without deduction of costs or expenses.

Guaranteed Issues. Bonds or stocks which are guaranteed as to principal, interest, dividends, sinking fund, etc., by a company other than the issuer. Guarantees usually come about through lease of the property of the issuing company to another company, or to facilitate the sale of securities by one company which is controlled by another. The value of the guarantee depends upon the credit standing and earnings of the guaranteeing company; but a guaranteed issue may stand on its own feet, even though the guarantee itself is questionable.

Hedge. Usually to make a commitment in commodities for future delivery in order to avoid risk of price change in such commodity entering into the cost of goods already contracted for manufacture and sale. In stock market operations, to purchase a senior convertible issue and sell short the amount of common stock obtainable if conversion privilege is exercised—(or other operations similar thereto).

Holding Company. A corporation which owns all or a majority of the stock of subsidiaries. The distinction sometimes made between a *holding company* and a *parent company* is that the latter is an operating company which also owns or controls other operating companies, whereas the holding company merely holds or controls operating companies.

House of Issue. Investment banking company engaged in the underwriting and distribution of security issues.

Idle Plant Expense. The cost of carrying (maintaining and allowing for depreciation on) nonoperating manufacturing properties.

Income Account. A report of operations over a specified period of time, summarizing the revenues or income and the expenses or costs attributed to that period, and indicating the net profit or loss for the period. Frequently called the *Profit & Loss Statement.*

Income Bonds. Bonds the payment at interest on which is dependent on earnings. In some bonds part of the interest is on a fixed basis and the balance is on an income or contingent basis. Income bonds are sometimes called adjustment bonds.

Indenture. The legal document prepared in connection with a bond issue setting forth the terms of the issue, its specific security, remedies in case of default, duties of the Trustee, etc. Also called the "deed of trust."

Intangible Assets. Capital (Fixed) Assets which are neither physical nor financial in character. Include patents, trademarks, copyrights, franchises, good-will, leaseholds and such deferred charges as unamortized bond discount. These assets should be shown on the balance sheet at cost, if at all, but frequently are assigned purely arbitrary values.

Intercorporate Debt. Debt of one corporation to another

corporation controlling it, controlled by it, or controlled by the same interests that control the debtor.

Interest Coverage. The number of times that interest charges are earned, found by dividing the (total) fixed charges into the earnings available for such charges (either before or after deducting income taxes).

Intrinsic Value. The "real value" behind a security issue, as contrasted with its market price. Generally a rather indefinite concept; but sometimes the balance sheet and earnings record supply dependable evidence that the intrinsic value is substantially higher or lower than the market price.

Inventories. Current assets representing the present stock of finished merchandise, goods in process of manufacture, raw materials used in manufacture, and sometimes miscellaneous supplies such as packing and shipping supplies. Usually stated at cost or market value, whichever is lower.

Investment Trust. The name given to an enterprise which invests its capital in a varied list of securities, intending to give its bond- and stock-holders the benefit of expert financial management and diversification. Really a misnomer, since practically all these enterprises are now corporations and not legal trusts; and also because many of the purchases may be of a speculative rather than an investment character.

Joint and Several Guarantee. A guarantee by more than one party under which each party is potentially liable for the full amount involved if his associates do not meet their share of the obligation.

Joint Facility Rents. In railroad income statements, represent rentals paid (dr.) or received (cr.) for terminal facilities or other similar properties used jointly by several railroads.

Junior Issue. An issue whose claim for interest or dividends, or for principal value, comes after some other issue, called a senior issue. Second mortgages are junior to first mortgages on the same property; common stock is junior to preferred stock, etc.

Leasehold. The right to occupy a property at a specified rental for a specified period of years. To obtain a long term lease at a favorable rental a cash bonus is frequently paid by the lessee to the lessor (owner), if it is a new lease, or to the former lessee, if the lease is taken over. The balance sheet item "Leaseholds" should represent only this cash consideration, and should be amortized over the life of the lease.

Leasehold Improvements. The cost of improvements or betterments to property leased for a period of years. Such improvements ordinarily become the property of the lessor (owner) on expiration of the lease; consequently their cost must be amortized over the life of the lease.

Leasehold Obligations. The obligation or liability, inherent in a Leasehold, to pay a specified rental for a specified period of years.

Legal Investments. Securities which conform with the regulations set up by legislative enactment governing the investments made by savings banks and trust funds in a given State. Usually the banking department of the State publishes annually a list of securities considered eligible for investment by savings banks and trust funds, commonly referred to as "legals."

Leverage. The condition making for wide changes in per share earnings and market value, arising from the fact that a company's common stock has relatively heavy fixed costs or deductions (interest and/or preferred dividends) ahead of it. Small percentage changes in gross earnings or operating costs will affect the earnings and market price of the common stock in much greater ratio. A leverage stock usually sells at a small aggregate figure in proportion to the total amount of senior securities.

Liabilities. Recognized claims against an enterprise. In its narrower sense includes only creditors' claims, i.e., excludes the claims of owners represented by the Capital

Stock, Surplus and Proprietorship Reserve accounts. In its broader sense, includes all items on the right side of the balance sheet.

Liability Reserve. A reserve or claim against an enterprise representing a liability the existence of which is unquestioned but the exact amount of which cannot as yet be determined (e.g., reserve for taxes).

Liquid Assets. Same as current assets; but sometimes applied to current assets excluding inventory.

Liquidating Value. The amount which would be available for a security if the business were wound up and the assets turned into cash. Is less than "book value," because allowance must be made for shrinkage in the value of the various kinds of assets if sold during a short period.

Maintenance. Upkeep and repair costs required to maintain plant and equipment in efficient operating condition.

Margin of Profit. Operating income divided by sales. Depreciation is usually included in the operating expenses while income taxes are usually excluded. Non-operating income received and interest charges paid are not included in arriving at the operating income.

Margin of Safety. In general the same as "interest coverage," which appears above. Formerly used in a special sense, to mean the ratio of the balance after interest to the earnings available for interest. Example: If interest is covered $1\frac{3}{4}$ times, the margin of safety (in this special sense) becomes $\frac{3}{4} \div 1\frac{3}{4} = 42\ 6/7\%$.

Marketability. The facility with which a security may be bought and sold. Good marketability requires a continuous close relation between bid and offering prices sufficient to permit ready purchase or sale in fair volume.

Merger. A combination in which one company absorbs one or more other companies.

Minority Interest. In a consolidated income statement, represents the interest or equity of the minority stockholders of a subsidiary in the earnings of that subsidiary. In a consolidated balance sheet, represents the interest or equity of these minority stockholders in the net worth of the subsidiary.

Mortgage, "Blanket." Usually the same as general mortgage. May be applied more specifically to a mortgage issue covering a number of separated properties.

Mortgage, General. A lien on all the fixed property of a corporation at the time of issuance, usually junior to underlying mortgages.

Mortgage, Guaranteed. A mortgage on real estate on which payment of principal or interest (usually both) is guaranteed by a Mortgage Guarantee Company or a Surety Company. Sometimes the whole mortgage is sold with the guarantee attached; frequently one or more mortgages are deposited with the trustee and "guaranteed mortgage certificates" are issued with the mortgage(s) as security.

Negotiable Instruments. Certain kinds of property—e.g., currency, checks, promissory notes, acceptances, coupon bonds—title to which passes on delivery and cannot be attacked when in the hands of a holder in due course and in good faith. Stocks are not negotiable instruments; hence stolen certificates may be recovered from an innocent holder.

Net Current Assets (Working Capital). Current assets less current liabilities.

Net Quick Assets. Either same as above, or (preferably) net current assets excluding inventory.

Net Plant. See Property Account.

Net Worth. The amount available for the stockholders as shown by the books. Is made up of capital, surplus, and such reserves as are equivalent to surplus. It is ordinarily used to include intangible assets as they appear on the books, and to that extent differs from the "book value" of the stock issues.

Non-Cumulative Preferred Stock. Preferred stock subject to the provision that if dividends are not declared in any period, the holder loses all rights to dividends for that period. Where the dividends are cumulative to the extent earned, the issue stands midway between a straight cumulative and a straight non-cumulative preferred.

Non-Detachable Warrants. See Warrants.

Non-Recurrent Items. Earnings or deductions from some special source not likely to appear in subsequent years. Such items should be separated from the regular earnings or deductions in analyzing a report. *Examples of non-recurrent earnings:* Profit on sales of capital assets; special dividends from subsidiaries; profit on bond retirement; amount received in settlement of litigation; etc. *Examples of non-recurrent deductions:* Loss on sale of capital assets; inventory write-off; idle plant expense (in some cases); etc.

Obsolescence. The loss of value of a capital asset resulting from new manufacturing developments or inventions which render the asset commercially unusable. Also, the accounting charge (usually part of the Depreciation charge) to adjust for the probable future loss in value resulting from these causes.

Operating Ratio. In the case of railroads, the ratio found by dividing total operating revenue (or "gross revenue") into operating expenses excluding taxes. In the case of public utilities, it is generally defined as the ratio of operating expenses including taxes and depreciation to the total revenue. Similarly in the case of industrials, except that some authorities do not include depreciation and most do not include income taxes in operating expenses.

Option Warrants. See Warrants.

Organization Expense. Direct costs of forming a new corporate enterprise: mostly incorporation fees and taxes and legal fees. May appear on the balance sheet as a Deferred Asset; if so, is usually written off against the first few years' earnings.

Over-All Method. The proper method of calculating bond interest or preferred dividend coverage. In the case of bond interest it means finding the number of times that *total fixed charges* are covered. In the case of preferred dividends it means finding the number of times that the aggregate of all *fixed charges plus preferred dividends* are covered. (In dealing with a preferred issue senior to another preferred issue, the requirements of the junior issue may be omitted.)

Parent Company. See Holding Company.

Participating Issues. Bonds (very infrequently) or preferred stocks which are entitled to additional interest or dividends, above the regular rate, depending either on (a) the amount of earnings, or (b) the amount of dividends paid on the common stock.

Plant Account. See Property Account.

"Preemptive Right." The right of shareholders to purchase additional shares or other securities (generally securities convertible into common stock) before these are sold to other purchasers. Preemptive rights are generally accorded stockholders under State laws, but may be waived in the charter or by-laws.

Preferred Stock. Stock which has a prior claim on dividends (and/or assets in the case of dissolution of the corporation) up to a certain definite amount before the common stock is entitled to anything. See Cumulative Preferred Stock, Non-Cumulative Preferred Stock, and Participating Issues.

Premium on Bonds. The excess of the market price of a bond, or the amount received by the issuer, over its face value.

Premium on Capital Stock. The excess of cash or equivalent received by the issuer over the par value of capital stock issued therefor.

Prepaid Assets. See Deferred Assets.

Price-Earnings Ratio. Market price divided by current annual earnings per share. Example: Stock selling at 84 and earning $7 per share has a price earnings ratio of 12 to 1 (or is said to be selling at 12 times earnings).

Prior Deductions Method. An entirely improper method of

calculating bond interest or preferred dividend coverage. The requirements of senior obligations are first deducted from earnings and the balance is applied to the requirements of the junior issue. See Over-All Method.

Prior Lien. A lien or mortgage ranking ahead of some other lien. A prior lien need not itself be a first mortgage.

Privileged Issue. A bond or preferred stock which has a conversion or participating right, or has a stock purchase warrant attached to it.

Profit & Loss Statement. See Income Statement.

Profit & Loss Surplus. See Surplus.

Property Account. The cost (or sometimes, the appraised value) of land, buildings, and equipment acquired to carry on business operations. *Net Property Account* represents cost or appraised value of these assets less accrued depreciation to date, i.e., property account less depreciation reserve. The terms *Plant* and *Net Plant* frequently are used with the same respective meanings, but sometimes exclude land or non-stationary assets such as delivery equipment.

Proprietorship Reserves. Reserves set up as segregations of Surplus, which serve merely to earmark part of the stockholders' equity as not subject to distribution in the form of cash dividends. Include most contingency reserves and also reserves for sinking funds and plant extensions. Represent, not liabilities, but equities.

Prospectus. A document describing a new security issue; especially, the detailed description which must be supplied to intending purchasers under the Securities Act of 1933.

Protective Committee. A committee, generally organized at the initiative of substantial holders of a given security, to act for all the owners of that security in important matters in difficulty or dispute. Most protective committees arise in connection with receivership and deal with the question of reorganization. Others may develop merely because of differences of opinion on some basic policy; e.g., between certain stockholders and the management.

Protective Covenants. Provisions in a bond indenture, or charter provisions affecting a preferred stock, (a) which bind the company not to do certain things considered injurious to the issue or, (b) which set forth remedies in the event of unfavorable developments. *Example of (a):* Agreement not to place a lien on the property ahead of the bond issue. *Example of (b):* The passing of voting power to the preferred stock if dividends are not paid.

Proxy. An authorization given by a security holder to someone else to vote his holdings for directors, or on some question put to vote.

Purchase Money Mortgages. Mortgages issued in partial payment for real estate or other property and having a lien on the property purchased. They are often used to circumvent the "after acquired property clause" in bonds which a company has previously issued.

"Pure Interest." The theoretical interest rate on a riskless investment. Varies with general credit conditions. The actual interest rate on a given investment is presumed to be made up of the pure interest rate, plus a premium to measure the risk taken.

Pyramiding. In stock market operations, the practice of using unrealized paper profits in marginal trading to make additional purchases. In corporate finance, the practice of creating a speculative capital structure by a series of holding companies, whereby a relatively small amount of voting stock in the parent company controls a large corporate system.

Qualitative Factors (in analysis). Considerations which cannot be stated in figures—such as management, strategic position, labor conditions, prospects, etc.

Quantitative Factors (in analysis). Considerations which can be stated in figures—such as balance sheet position, earnings record, dividend rate, capitalization set-up, production statistics, etc.

Quick Assets. (a) Sometimes used to mean current assets, but (b) preferably current assets excluding inventory.

Receivership. The operation of a company by an agent of the court, under direction of the court, usually arising from inability to meet obligations as they mature. There are technical differences between (a) an equity receivership, (b) a bankruptcy receivership, and (c) a trusteeship under Sections 77 and 77B of the Bankruptcy Act as amended.

Registration Statement. The forms filed by a corporation (or foreign governmental body) with the Securities and Exchange Commission in connection with an offering of new securities or the listing (registration) of outstanding securities on a national securities exchange. The "prospectus," supplied to intending purchasers of a new issue, contains most, but not all, of the information given in the registration statement.

Reserves. Offsets against total or specific asset values, set up on the books (a) to reduce or revalue assets, (b) to indicate the existence of liabilities generally of uncertain amount, or (c) to earmark part of Surplus for some future use. See Valuation Reserves, Liability Reserves, and Proprietorship Reserves. Properly speaking, *reserves* represent, not assets, but claims against or deductions from assets. Assets set aside to take care of reserves should be called "reserve *funds.*"

Restricted Shares. Common stock issued under an unusual agreement whereby they do not rank for dividends until some event has happened—usually the reaching of a certain level of earnings.

Retirement Expense or Retirement Reserve. (a) In the income account: The accounting charge, used by many concerns in lieu of Depreciation, for accruing loss due to ultimate retirement (scrapping) of operating equipment. May take into account all equipment owned, in which case it would approximate normal depreciation charges. More commonly, takes into account only equipment likely to be retired within the next few years, and hence is usually lower than normal depreciation charges. (b) In the balance sheet: Retirement Reserve is a valuation reserve representing accrued Retirement Expense to date. Similar to Depreciation Reserve, for which it is supposed to be a substitute, but frequently represents a smaller proportion of the value of the pertinent assets than would a properly built up depreciation reserve.

Revenue Expenditures. Expenditures or outlays of cash or its equivalent which are undertaken to maintain asset values (e.g., repairs, but not improvements) or to obtain current revenue (e.g., raw material purchases, factory labor payroll). Cf. Capital Expenditures.

Right. A privilege accorded to each unit of an existing security to purchase new securities. Generally must be exercised within a short time and is offered at a price under the existing market. (See Warrant.)

Royalty. A payment made (a) for the use of a patent, (b) to the owner of oil or gas lands by those extracting oil or gas therefrom, or (c) to the author of a book, play, etc.

Scrip Dividends. Dividends payable in notes or other written promises to pay the amount involved in cash at a later date. The date may be fixed, or contingent on certain happenings, or entirely discretionary with the directors.

Seasonal Variations or Fluctuations. Changes in operating results due to the time of the year. Allowance must be made for these in interpreting the results shown over part of the year.

Seasoned Issues. Securities of established large companies which have been favorably known to the investment public for a period of years covering good times and bad.

Secular Trend. A long term movement—e.g., of prices, production, etc.—in some definite direction. Opposed to seasonal fluctuations or variations.

Segregation. Separation from a holding or operating company of one or more of its subsidiaries or operating divisions, effected by distributing stock of the subsidiary to the shareholders of the parent company.

Senior Issue. See Junior Issue.

Serial Bonds. A bond issue providing that certain portions thereof mature on successive dates instead of all at once. Serial maturities are usually spaced one year apart.

Short Sale. Sale of a stock which is not owned. Delivery to purchaser is arranged by borrowing the stock from an owner who receives as security cash in amount equal and kept equal to the market price. Upon ultimate purchase of the stock by the short-seller, the certificate thereby received is turned over to the lender and cash posted with him returned.

Sinking Fund. An arrangement under which a portion of a bond or preferred stock issue is retired periodically in advance of its fixed maturity. The company may either purchase a stipulated quantity of the issue itself, or supply funds to a trustee or agent for the purpose. Retirement may be made by call at a fixed price, or by inviting tenders, or by purchase in the open market. The amount of the sinking fund may be fixed in dollars, or as a percentage of the issue, or be based upon volume of production or earnings.

Sliding Scale Privilege. A conversion or stock purchase privilege in which the price changes (almost always unfavorably to the senior issue) either with the passage of time or upon exercise of the privilege by a given amount of the issue.

Speculation. Financial transactions involving acknowledged risk entered into with the purpose of profiting from anticipated future events.

Split-Up. Division of a corporation's share capital into a greater number of share units, usually (in the case of shares having a par value) by reduction in the par value represented by each share. Thus, a split-up might consist of the issue, in exchange for each share of $100 par common stock outstanding, or four new $25 par common shares. Sometimes the reverse procedure is resorted to, i.e., the share capital is consolidated into a fewer number of shares by issuing only a fraction of a new share in exchange for each old share outstanding. For lack of a better title, this is frequently referred to as a *Reverse Split-Up* or *Split-Down*.

Stock Value Ratio. (a) In the case of a bond, the ratio of the total market value of the capital stock of a corporation to the par value of its funded debt. (b) In the case of a preferred stock, the ratio of the total market value of the common stock issues to the total par value of all the bonds plus the total market value of the preferred stock.

Stated Value (of Capital Stock). Value at which no-par capital stock is carried on the balance sheet. May be a purely arbitrary or nominal amount, or the issue price, or the book value of the stock. (In some states, par-value shares may be given a stated value less than their par.)

Stock Dividends. Dividends payable in the form of stock of the declaring company, but not necessarily of the same class as the shares receiving the stock dividend.

Stock Purchase Warrant. See Warrants.

Straight Investment. A bond or preferred stock, definitely limited in interest or dividend rate, purchased solely for its income return and without reference to possible increase in value.

Subsidiary. A company controlled by another company (called the Parent Company) through ownership of at least a majority of its voting stock.

Surplus. The excess of the total Net Worth or stockholders' equity over the total of par or stated value of the capital stock and the amount of Proprietorship Reserves. At least part of this excess usually results from earnings retained in the business; this part frequently is labeled *Earned Surplus* or *Profit & Loss Surplus*, to indicate its source. That part of surplus arising from other sources (e.g., write-ups of fixed asset values, write-downs of the par or stated value of capital stock issues, or sale of stock at a premium) frequently is labeled *Capital Surplus*.

Surplus Statement. A financial report summarizing the changes in Surplus during the fiscal year (or other period). Shows surplus at beginning of period, plus net income for the period, less dividends declared, plus or minus any extraordinary credits to or charges against surplus. Final item of report, consequently, is surplus at end of period. Report also called *Statement of Surplus* and *Analysis of Surplus*.

Switching. The process of selling a presently owned security and replacing it by another, to gain some expected advantage.

Tangible Assets. Assets either physical or financial in character—e.g. plant, inventory, cash, receivables, investments. See Intangibles.

Tax Free Covenant. An agreement by a corporation to pay interest without deduction of federal taxes that may be required to be withheld by law, usually up to a certain maximum percentage. By special provision of the income tax laws, the covenant means that corporations will pay income taxes up to two percent of the amount of the coupons.

Time Deposit. Money on deposit with a bank withdrawable at the end of a (short) period instead of on demand, and generally drawing interest.

Treasury Stock. Lawfully issued stock that has been reacquired by the corporation through purchase or donation.

Trend. A persistent change (e.g., of earnings) in a certain direction over a given period. Caution must be used in projecting a past earnings trend into the future.

Trustee. One to whom the title to property has been conveyed, for the benefit of another party. Thus the trustee for a mortgage bond issue holds the mortgage (i.e., has conveyed to it the mortgaged property) for the benefit, primarily of the bondholders. The trustee in bankruptcy holds title to the bankrupt's property (with certain exceptions) for the benefit primarily of the bankrupt's creditors. A trustee may also assume obligations not connected with the direct holding of property—e.g., a trustee under the indenture of an unsecured (debenture) bond.

Trustee Shares. See Bankers Shares.

Trust Funds. Funds held by a trustee for the benefit of another. Terms set forth by the creator of the trust govern the type of property in which the trustee may invest, whether restricted to "Legal Investments" or left to the discretion of the trustee.

Unamortized Bond Discount. That part of the original Bond Discount which has not as yet been amortized, or charged off against earnings.

Underlying Bonds. See Bonds, Underlying.

Unexpended Depreciation. See Depreciation.

Valuation Reserves. Reserves set up (a) to indicate a diminution in the value of the assets to which they pertain, or (b) to provide for a reasonably probable failure to realize full value. Example of (a): Depreciation and depletion reserves; reserve to reduce securities owned to market value. Example of (b): Reserve for bad accounts.

Voting Trust. An arrangement by which stockholders turn over their voting rights (generally for directors only) to a small group of individuals called voting trustees. The original stock certificates are registered in the name of the voting trustees and held in trust, the stockholders receiving instead other certificates called "voting trust certificates," (abbreviation v.t.c). Voting trusts generally run for five years. They usually give the holders all the privileges of the deposited securities, except that of voting.

Warrants. (a) Stock Purchase Warrants or Option Warrants. A right to purchase shares of stock, generally running for a longer period of time than the ordinary subscription "rights" given shareholders. These warrants are often attached to other securities, but they may be issued separately or detached after issuance. Non-detachable warrants cannot be dealt in separately from the security with which they were issued, and can only be exercised upon presentation with the original security. Option warrants are often issued in reorganizations or granted to management as additional compensation arîd incentive. (b) A name given to certain kinds of municipal obligations.

Wasting Assets. Tangible Fixed Assets subject to depletion through gradual removal in the normal course of operation of the business. (e.g. metal, oil, or sulphur deposits; timber lands.)

Watered Stock. Stock with real net asset value considerably less than its par or stated value, because some of the asset value included in the company's balance sheet is either fictitious or highly questionable.

"When Issued." A term applied to dealings in securities proposed to be issued under some reorganization, merger, or new capitalization scheme. The full descriptive phrase is "when, as, and if issued." If the plan is abandoned, or changed materially, the "when issued" trades are void.

Working Capital. The net current assets. Found by deducting current liabilities from the current assets.

Yield. The return on an investment, expressed as a percentage of cost. *Straight Yield* or *Current Yield* is found by dividing the market price into the dividend rate in dollars (for stocks) or interest rate (for bonds). It ignores the factor of maturity or possible call at a price higher or lower than the market. *Amortized Yield* or *Yield to Maturity* (of a bond) takes into account the eventual gain or loss of principal value to be realized through repayment at maturity. Where a bond is callable before maturity, the amortized yield might be lower if it is assumed that call takes place. The true amortized yield should be the lowest shown on any assumption as to call.

FINIS